PHYSICAL AND HEALTH EDUCATION

For B.Ed, B.P.Ed , M.P.Ed & NEP Degree Courses

Ravikumar N G

PHYSICAL AND HEALTH EDUCATION

Ravikumar N G

DEDICATION

To the past that shaped me, the present that nurtures me,
and the future that awaits me.

ACKNOWLEDGMENTS

A deep sense of gratitude and heartfelt thanks to Sri. B.Y. Raghavendra, Secretary, Swamy Vivekananda Vidya Samsthe (R), Shikaripura and Member of Parliament, Shivamogga Constituency for his guidance and encouragement to complete this Book.

I thank to Dr. Shivakumar G. S., Principal of Kumadvathi College of Education, Shikaripura and all the Teaching Staff and Non-Teaching Staff of Kumadvathi College of Education for their kind support and cooperation to write this book.

I extended my thanks all the Heads, Teaching Staff and Non-Teaching Staff of Swamy Vivekananda Vidya Samsthe (R), Shikaripura for their kind cooperation to write this book.

I am grateful to my parents and family members for their moral support.

I want to thank EVERYONE who ever said anything positive to me or taught me something. I heard it all, and it meant something.

I want to thank God most of all, because without God I wouldn't be able to do any of this.

CONTENTS

UNIT-1

I INTRODUCTION TO PHYSICAL EDUCATION

1.1 Meaning, Definition, Aim and Objectives of Physical Education.

1.2 Relationship of Physical Education with General Education.

1.3 Physical Fitness- Meaning, Definition, Components and Benefits of Physical Fitness.

1.4 Olympic games - Origin and Development of Modern Olympic games. Objectives of Modern Olympic games.

1.1 MEANING, DEFINITION, AIM AND OBJECTIVES OF PHYSICAL EDUCATION.

Physical Education

The word physical education comprises of two words Physical and Education. The plain dictionary meaning of word physical as relating to body characteristics of a person such as physical strength, physical endurance, physical fitness physical appearance or physical health. The word education may mean the systematic instructions or training or preparation for some particular tasks. The two words combined together stands for the systematic instructions or training related to physical activities or programme of activities necessary for development and maintenance of human body or the development of physical powers or activities for cultivating physical skills.

Definition of Education

In the modern context physical education has been recognised as an integral part of general education. It is necessary to have basic knowledge regarding the topic education itself. Therefore, this unit deals with the vital issues concerning education and projects various facets of education as well.

Swamy Vivekananda - 'Education is the manifestation of perfection already in man'.

Shri Aurobindo - "The chief aim of education should be to help the growing soul to draw out that in itself, which is best and make it perfect for a noble use."

M.K. Gandhi - 'By Education I mean an all-round drawing out of the best in child and man, body, mind and spirit.

Rabindra Nath Tagore - That education is highest which not only imparts information and knowledge to us, but also promotes love and fellow-feeling between us, and the living beings of the world.

Aristotle - Education develops man's faculty, especially his mind, so that he may be able to enjoy the contemplation of supreme truth, goodness and beauty, in which perfect happiness essentially consists.

Pestalozzi - Education is the natural, harmonious and progressive development of man's innate.

Shankaracharya - The ultimate aim of education is to prepare the child for the realisation of salivation.

A.S. Atekar - Education has always been regarded in India as a source of illumination and power which transforms and ennobles our nature by the progressive and harmonious development of our physical, mental, intellectual and spiritual power and faculties.

The ultimate goal sought to be achieved through education can be said to be the aim of education. An aim revolves around a center of purpose, it is abstract, never fully realised, and represents ideal. It must present a challenge to the educationists and students alike. It must the have the power to inspire towards greater effort. Aim of education is the hub of wheel around which all other purposes of education revolve. It serves as a thread that can bring all valid purposes of education into an integrated whole.

Swami Dayananda in his book **'Satyartha Prakash'** has stated that the ultimate aim of of education is to lead towards liberation through development of character.

Meaning and Definition of Physical Education

Generally, physical1 education is misunderstood to mean physical activity or merely drill. It is necessary to provide knowledge regarding true meaning and scope of physical education. The aims and objectives of physical education are also being stated in detail so as to enable the students to understand the basic concept of the subject. It is also pertinent to deal with the controversy whether physical education is an art or science.

Meaning of Physical Education

The word physical education is derived from two separate words, **"physical'** and **'education.** The plain dictionary meaning of word physical is **'relating to body',** it may relate to any one or all of the bodily characteristics. It may be physical strength, physical endurance, physical fitness, physical appearance or physical health. The word 'education' means systematic instructions or training, or preparation for life or for some particular task. A combined meaning of these two words would be that systematic instructions or training which relate to physical activities or programme of activities, necessary for development and maintenance of human body, development of physical powers, or cultivation of physical skill.

Education is a "doing"' phenomenon, one learns through doing. Education is not confined to class-room alone, it may take place on the play-ground, in library, or even at home. Such an education is conducive to the enrichment of an individual's life. A well-directed programme of physical education leads to healthy living, social efficacy, good physical health, and worthy use of leisure time. In the modern context, the term physical education has assumed much broader and more meaningful application to our daily life. Physical education is the education of man in' and by' means of physical activity. It is education of physical through physical. Physical education is that education which starts with physical development and advances towards per ect development of human being, the ultimate result being vigorous and strong body, acquisition of sound health, mental alertness, and social and emotional balance. Such an individual will be able to interpret new situations effectively, in more meaningful and purposeful manner and can be said to be a Physically Educated Person".

Definition of Physical Education

Definitions change with the ideas that express people's notions of values, of importance, of measures, and of life. It is therefore not possible to give one definition of physical education. Different physical educationists have given different definitions.

Harold M. Barrow - Physical education is an education of and through human movement where many of the educational objectives are achieved by means of big muscle activities involving sport, games, gymnas tics, dance, and exercises.

Jay B. Nash - Physical education is that phase of the whole field of education that deals with big muscle activities and their rela ted responses.

Cassidy - 'Physical education is the sum of the changes in the individual caused by experiences cantering motor activity'.

Charles A. Bucher - Physical education, an integral part of the total education process, is a field of endeavour that has as its aim the improvement of human performance through the medium of physical activities that have been selected with a view to realizing this outcome.

Delbert Oberteuffer - Physical education is the sum of those experiences which come to the individual through movement.

J.P. Thomas - 'Physical Education is education through physical activities to the evelopment of total personality of the child and its fulfilment and perfection in body mind and spirit'.

William H. Kilpatrick - Physical education is a way of ducation through motor activities and related experiences and its subject atter is primarily ways of behaving.

Thomas Wood- The great thought in physical education is not the education of the physical nature, but the relation of physical training to complete education.

Aims of Physical Education

The most remote goal is referred to as an aim, it charts direction, it points the way. The aim should be general in character and beyond realisation so that it can serve continually as a goal, as Browning's lines suggest.

The aim, however, should not be visionary but a practical way of indicating purpose.

He had indicated a purpose, a direction, and yet the aim will never be realised; there will always be better opportunities that can be provided. As far back as in 1983 Thomas Wood had stated Physical education must have an aim as broad as education itself and as noble and inspiring as human life".

J.R. Sherman - The aim of physical education is to influence the experiences of persons to the extent that each individual within the limitsof his capacity may be helped to adjust successfully in society, to increase and improve his wants, and to develop the ability to satisfy his wants."

Objective of Physical Education

The objectives of physical education are stated differently by many of Physical Educationists. The following are main objectives of physical education.

Development of Organic Fitness: This objective deals with the program of activities which builds physical power in and individual through the development of the various organic systems of the body. The systems such a circulatory system, respiratory system, nervous system, muscular system and digestive systems. Physical education is related to physical activities, which create various effects on our organic systems. These systems are developed in size, shape, efficiency etc. This promotes a sound health, which enables the individual to be the valuable asset for the nation. If our systems remain in sound health, they can perform their functions in an efficiency way.

Development of Mental health: The mental development objective deals with the accumulation of a body of knowledge and the ability to think and to interpret their knowledge. Physical education programmers need alertness of mind, deep concentration and calculated movements. Physical activities sharpen the mind, to perform various activities. It includes rules and regulations techniques of games, anatomical and physiological studies balanced diet, sanitation, health and diseases personal hygiene etc. Through participation in various activities an individual learns to draw certain conclusions. He is able to understand the new situations faced in the games. He is able to take decisions independently.

Social Development: In the democratic society in which we live it is necessary to have all individual develop sense of group consciousness and cooperative living. Social traits are essential for better adjustment in life. The programme of physical education develops these traits. They provide leadership qualities. Through physical activities, the players come closer with each other and adjust themselves according to situations. It helps in attaining the traits like cooperation courtesy fair play, sportsmanship self-control unselfishness tolerance and sympathy.

Development of Neuro muscular co-ordination: The nervous system is strengthened only proper physical exercise. neuro muscular coordination develops well only of various of exercises are done repeated for a long period of time. Good neuro muscular coordination helps to keep off fatigue coordination. We get accuracy and smooth function of our body. Our reaction time becomes less. Neuro muscular development helps ones be perform the daily work with proficiency develops a well poised quick and efficient movement and body graceful carriage.

Development of Desirable habits

> To be inculcated regular activities rest regulated diet
>
> Maintaining cleanliness
>
> To be disciplined in one's work
>
> Chalking out a schedule of desirable activities that may
>
> contribute towards a healthy body and a happy mind

Development of Personality

Attainment of sportsmanship

Development of leadership qualities

Development of social cooperation

Development of fearlessness

Attainment of positive qualities of self confidence

Attainment of self-control

Providing for Mental Hygiene

Mental Hygiene comprises those activities and techniques which promote and maintain mental health.

Development of ability to face stresses and string of like

Elimination of worry and tension through games and sports

Development of Functional Knowledge

To know the rules and techniques of different games

To know and acquire knowledge, proper health procedure

To know the methods and principles of games and exercises

To know the body parts and the effects of exercise on various organs and systems.

Development of qualities of a good citizenship

One has to abide rules and regulation

One's discipline improves the qualities of a good citizenship

Scope of Physical Education

Physical Education as an integral part of general education- through activity oriented and well planned programmes they organize different physical activities like drill and marching etc which are directed towards physical, mental emotional, social, intellectual and moral development of the child. The following are the scope of physical education.

Corrective Exercises: Corrective exercises help to remove the deformities in the body of a child. Sometimes these defects are there because of defects in muscle development and for the we use light corrective exercises.

Games and Sports: various team games like hockey foot ball, cricket basketball and volley ball etc and individual events like athletics, wrestling, boxing judo and archy are included in the programmers of physical education. Swimming, diving, canoeing etc are related to water sports.

Rhythmics: Gymamstics, Leziums Dance, mass physical training and Dumb bell etc. are rhythmical activities necessary for rhythm and balance. Rhythmical activities are also included in the programmes of physical education.

Self-defense activities: Hiking, Trekking, Judo, karate and self-defense activities are included in the programmes of physical education.

Recreational activities: Recreational activities like minor games, chess, carom, horse riding, education campus, hunting, folk dance, fishing etc are included in the programems of physical education.

Yogic activities: Yogic activities such as Asana Pranayama Kiryas etc are included in Physical education.

On the basis of the above mentioned facts, the following activities can be included in a programme of physical education India:

Free hand exercises, Exercises with apparatus, Major games, Minor games, Gymnastics, Track and field events, Folk dances, Yoga, Rhythmic, Combative, Swimming and diving, Hiking trekking camping etc, Pyramids, Dands and baithaks.

Importance of Physical Education

- Physical education develops the alertness of mind.

- Physical education provides knowledge about health and its hazards and communicable and non-communicable diseases.

- Through physical activities leisure time can be utilized properly

- Through physical education human body can be developed in good proportion. The physical beauty also improves

- A good sports man is a good citizen He knows how to adjust with others

- Physical education helps in developing and maintaining of good relations among humans beings. It develops social traits, like cooperation, sympathy, loyalty, fraternity, courtesy and other traits of leadership.

- Aggressiveness can be eliminated through physical activities. By participating physical activities, we can overcome stress tension and sensitiveness

- Physical education helps in creating discipline through games and sports

- Physical education provides a numbers of opportunities to enhance the power of tolerance

- Physical education enhances all the essential traits required for development of the personality

- Physical education leads to happiness efficiency and character building

- Physical education helps the people to become fit to develop their spiritual and more forces. It increases the scope of human abilities and enriches the life of the individual and that of the society as a whole.

1.2 RELATIONSHIP OF PHYSICAL EDUCATION WITH GENERAL EDUCATION.

Physical education has long been recognized as an integral part of the total process of education. Man is an indivisible integration of body, mind and soul, and education must attempt to strengthen this integration. The whole man should have a whole education. Any narrow interpretation of term education' so as to mean curriculum followed in school, extent of schooling or development of intellectual aspect alone would defeat the very purpose of education. No individual, no community, no nation can depend upon one aspect of life for the whole of living. Man is a psycho-physical organism and mind and body should not be conceived as two separate entities. It has been very appropriately summed up by Montaigne, it is not a soul, it is not a body that we are training up; It is a man, and we ought not to divide him into two parts". John Locke also expressed similar thought by stating, "A sound mind in a sound body is a short but full description of a happy state in this world."

There has been a significant shift in the definition of education from the 3Rs (reading writing, arithmetic) to 3 Ms (man, material, method) i.e. all-round development of personality. It clearly establishes that physical education is an integral part of general education. A Bucher is also of the same view. He defined "physical education as an integral part of the total education process".

It is by now well accepted that growth and development of an individual is the real essence of education. According to Swami Vivekananda "the end result of all education, all training should be man making'" Modern education has recognised its responsibility of 'man making by undertaking the development of all the aspect of personality i.e. mental, physical, emotional, intellectual, and social, the end result being all- round development of the personality. Physical education also strives to achieve the same end result.

"Physical education is education through physical activities for the development of total personality of the child and its fulfillment and perfection in body, mind and spirit." J.P. Thomas

Physical education is a process through which wholesome development of the child is ensured. The first lesson of education that a child learns is through body movements. D. Oberteuffer endorsed similar views and said, Physical education is the sum of those experiences which come to the individual through movements." These initial body movements of the child are followed by play.

"Play is the natural unfolding of the germinal leaves of childhood. "
-Froebel

Play is an inherent tendency and a gift of nature. Infact, play is nature's prescribed course of education and helps the child to grow physically, mentally, emotionally, and socially by providing freedom, spontaneity and self-expression, highlighting the educational importance of play.

"The disco very of the educational possibilities of the play side of life may be counted one of the greatest discoveries of the present day. It marks, I am convinced, the dawn of a new era in human education...... All over the civilized world today, education for leisure is challenging the attention of thoughtful men.... The liberal education of the body is the education of the mind as well." -L.P. Jacks

Play field serves as a small class-room, a laboratory with many educational processes going on which provide knowledge, liberate the mind, improve the skill, promote free thinking. encourage creative talent and development of positive attitudes. It is here that the child gets an opportunity of exposure to learned and shared behavior which result in his total development.

"The aim of physical education is the optimum development of physically, socially, and mentally integrated and adjusted individuals.".
-Book Walter

It can be concluded that the aims of general education and physical education are identical and directed towards same direction i.e. total and harmonious development of an individual.

Even the objectives of education are compatible and in harmony with the objectives of physical education. By acquiring an inquiring mind, by teaching philosophy of life. by self-expression and by appreciation by one's own body, physical education can contribute to self- realisation objective of education. Physical education through its varied activities provide rich opportunities of socialization, to develop cohesion, cooperation and leadership qualities which all foster the feeling of good human relationship, another objective of education. Physical education contributes to economic efficiency, the third objective of education, by teaching that one's success in profession or in profession or vocation depends upon his health and fitness state. Fourth objective of education, civic responsibility, is realised through physical education by inculcating qualities of good citizenship, leadership, patriotism, humane- tarantism and by teaching obedience of laws.

Physical education also transmits social and cultural values, and ideologies of the society to the younger generation enabling their absorption into the society by providing continuity in action and thought. It helps the child not only to grow and develop physically but to learn to fit into the social environment and make positive adjustments in his mental, social and physical responses. Physical education with its emphasis upon free and spontaneous play in childhood. vigorous rhythmic movements in adolescent and recreation activities for older people may hold the key to life.

Physical education is an indispensable area of education as it contributes to the health, to the social, emotional and mental development of an individual. In the modern hi-tech society, we cannot undermine the importance of relationship between general education and physical education. These are complementary and supplementary to each other. Their aims and objectives lead towards common goal – the all-round development of personality, enabling the man to lead enriched, abundant and harmonious life. Therefore, physical education is an integral part of general education and their relationship cannot be ignored. They are inter- related and inter-dependent, and constitute an indivisible whole

1.3 PHYSICAL FITNESS- MEANING, DEFINITION, COMPONENTS AND BENEFITS OF PHYSICAL FITNESS.

Today, there is a growing emphasis on looking good, feeling good and living longer, increasingly, scientific evidence tells us that one of the keys to achieving these ideals is fitness and exercises. Getting moving is a challenge because today physical activity is less a part of or daily lives. There are fewer jobs that require physical exertion. We have become a mechanically mobile society, relying on machines rather than muscles to get around. In addition, we have become a nation of observers with more people (including children) spending their problem leisure time pursuing just that – leisure. Consequently, statistics show that obesity and overweight, the problems that come with high blood pressure, diabetes, cardiac arrest, etc. are on the rise. But statistics also show that preventive medicine pays off, so one should not wait until his/her doctor gives an ultimatum. Everyone must take the initiative to get active now.

The decision to carry out a physical fitness program cannot be taken lightly. It requires a lifelong commitment of time and effort. Exercise must become one of those things that you do without question, like bathing and brushing your teeth. Unless you are convinced of the benefits of fitness and the risks of unfitness, you will not succeed. It has been realized that fitness adds not only years to one's life, but life to one's years.

Patience is essential. Don't try to do too much too soon and don't quit before you have a chance to experience the rewards of improved fitness. You can't regain physical fitness in a few days or weeks what you have lost in years of sedentary living, but you can get it back if you persevere.

In the following section you will find the basic information you need to begin and maintain a personal physical fitness programme. These guidelines are intended for the average healthy adult. It tells you what your goals should be a how often, how long and how hard you must exercise to achieve them. It also includes information that will make your workouts easier, safer and more satisfying. The rest is up to you.

Definitions of Physical Fitness

Physical fitness is to the human body what fine-tuning is to an engine. It enables us to perform up to our potential. Fitness can be described as a condition that helps us for better look, pleasant feel and do our best. More specifically, it is: "The ability to perform daily tasks vigorously and alertly, with energy left over for enjoying leisure-time activities and meeting emergency demands. It is the ability to endure, to bear up, to withstand stress, to carry on in circumstances where an unfit person could not continue, and is a major basis for good health and well-being."

"Physical fitness refers to the organic capacity of the individual to perform the normal task of daily living without undue tiredness or fatigue having reserves of strength and energy available to meet satisfactorily any emergency demands suddenly place upon him." Nixon

"Fitness is that state which characterizes the degree to which the person able to function. Fitness is an individual matter. It implies the ability of each person to live most effectively with his potential. Ability to function depends upon physical, mental, emotional and social components of fitness, all of which are related to each other and mutually interdependent." Kirchner

Physical fitness involves the performance of the heart and lungs, and the muscles of the body. And, since what we do with our bodies also affects what we can do with our minds, fitness influences to some degree qualities such as mental alertness and emotional stability.

As you undertake your fitness programme, it's important to remember that fitness is an individual quality that differs from person to person. It is influence by age, sex, heredity, personal habits, exercise and eating habits, diet, attitude towards life, anxiety, tension and stress, values of physical fitness, institutional curricular and state's policy/legislation, you can't do anything about the first three factors. However, it is within your power to change and improve the others where needed.

Components of Physical Fitness:

Exercise scientists have identified nine elements/components that comprise the definition of fitness. The following lists each of the nine elements and an example of how they are used:

Strength – the extent to which muscles can exert force by contracting against resistance (holding or restraining an object or person).

Power – the ability to exert maximum muscular contraction instantly in an explosive burst of movements (jumping or sprint starting)

Speed – the quickness of movement of limb, whether this is the leg of a runner or the arm of the shot putter.

Agility – the ability to perform a series of explosive power movement in rapid succession in opposing direction (Zigzag running or cutting movements).

Balance – the ability to control the body's position, either stationary (e.g. a handstand) or while moving (e.g. a gymnastics stunt)

Flexibility – the ability to achieve an extended range of motion without being impeded by excess tissue, i.e. fat or muscles (Executing a leg split).

Local Muscle Endurance – a single muscle's ability to perform sustained work (Rowing or cycling)

Cardiovascular Endurance – the heart ability to deliver blood to working muscles and their ability to use it (Running long distances)

Strength Endurance – a muscle's ability to perform a maximum contracture time after time (Continuous explosive rebounding through an entire basketball game).

Co-ordination – the ability to integrate the above listed components so that effective movements are achieved.

Physical fitness is the most easily understood by examining these components, or elements, or "parts". There is widespread agreement that following four elements are basic.

1) Endurance – the ability to deliver oxygen and nutrients to tissues, and to remove wastes, over sustained periods of time. Long runs and swims are among the methods employed in measuring this component.

2) Strength – the ability of a muscle to exert force for a brief period of time. Upper-body strength, for example, can be measured by various weight-lifting exercises.

3) Speed – the quickness of movement of limb, whether this is the leg of a runner or the arm of the shot putter.

4) Flexibility – the ability to move joints and use muscles through their full range of motion. The sit and reach test is a good measure of flexibility of the lower back and backs of the upper legs.

Body composition is also considered a component of fitness. It refers to the makeup of the body in terms of lean mass (muscle, bone, vital tissue and organs) and fat mass. An optimal ratio of fat to lean mass is an indication of fitness, and the right types of exercise will help you decrease body fat and increase or maintain muscles mass.

Benefits of Physical Fitness

Exercise or fitness is not just for Olympic hopefuls or supermodels. In fact, you are never too unfit, too young or too old to get started. Regardless of your age, gender or role in life, you can benefit from regular physical activity. If you are committed, exercise in combination with a sensible diet can help to provide an overall sense of well-being and can even help to prevent chronic illness, disability and premature death. Some of the benefits of increased physical activity or physical fitness are:

Improved Health

- Increased efficiency of heart and lungs
- Reduced cholesterol levels
- Increased muscle strength
- Reduced blood pressure
- Reduced risk of major illnesses such as diabetes and heart disease
- Weight loss

Improved Sense of Well-being

- More energy
- Less stress
- Improved quality of sleep
- Improved ability to cope with stress
- Increased mental sharpness

Improved Appearance

- Weight loss
- Toned muscles
- Improved posture
- Enhanced Social Life
- Improved Self-image
- Increased opportunities to make new friends

- Increased opportunities to share an activity with friends or family members

Increased Stamina

- Increased productivity
- Increased physical capabilities
- Less frequent injuries
- Less frequent injuries
- Improved immunity to minor illnesses.

Development of Physical Fitness

By improving the basic components physical fitness such as endurance, strength, speed and agility (coordinative ability) one can develop physical fitness. These elements can be developed through different means/methods of training. Beforehand, one must know about warming and cooling down and its importance.

Endurance

The objective of endurance training is to develop the energy production system(s) to meet the demands of the event. Endurance can be developed using continuous and interval running.

Energy Production Systems

In the human body, food energy is used to make adenosine triphosphate (ATP) the chemical compound that supplies energy for muscular contraction. Since ATP is in very low concentrations in the muscle, and it decreases only to a minor extent, tightly controlled energy pathways exist for the constant regeneration of ATP as muscular contraction continues. For continuous exercise, ATP must be re-**synthesized at the same rate as it is utilized.**

Types of endurance: The types of endurance are:

1) Aerobic endurance
2) Anaerobic endurance

3) Speed endurance

4) Strength endurance

A sound basis of aerobic endurance is fundamental for all events.

Aerobic Endurance:

Aerobic means 'with oxygen'. During aerobic work the body is working at a level that the demands for oxygen and fuel can be met by the body's intake. The only waster products formed are carbon dioxide and water. These are removed as sweat and by breathing out.

Aerobic endurance can further be sub-divided as follows:

- Short aerobic – 2 minutes to 8 minutes (lactic/aerobic)
- Medium aerobic – 8 minutes to 30 minutes (mainly aerobic)
- Long aerobic – 30 minutes + (aerobic) –
- Aerobic endurance is developed through the use of
- Duration runs to improve maximum oxygen uptake (VO2max)
- Interval training to improve the heart as a muscular pump.
- This can be achieved through different aerobic activities or exercises.

Aerobic Exercise

The American College of Sports Medicine (ACSM) defines aerobic exercise as "any activity that uses large muscle groups, can be maintained continuously, and is rhythmic in nature". It is a type of exercise that overloads the heart and lungs and causes them to work harder than at rest. The important idea behind aerobic exercise today, is to get up and get moving!! There are more activities than ever to choose from, whether it is a new activity or an old one. Find something you enjoy doing that keeps your heart rate high for a continuous time period and get moving to a healthier life.

Types of Aerobic Exercise

1) Aerobic Dance

2) Waling for Fitness

3) Rope Skipping

4) Running
5) Stair Climbing
6) Swimming
7) Bicycling
8) Cross Country

Anaerobic endurance

Anaerobic means 'without oxygen'. During anaerobic work, involving maximum effort, the body is working so hard that the demands for oxygen and fuel go above the rate of supply and the muscles have to really on the stored reserved of fuel. In this case waster products gather, the main one being lactic acid. The muscles, being hungry of oxygen, take the body into a state known as oxygen debt.

The body's stored fuel soon runs out and activity ceases painfully. Activity will not be resumed until the lactic acid is removed and the oxygen debt repaid. Fortunately, the body can resume limited activity after even only a small amount of the oxygen debt has been repaid. Since lactic acid is produced the correct term for this pathway is lactic anaerobic energy pathway. The lactic anaerobic pathway is the one in which the body is working anaerobically but without the production of lactic acid. This pathway can exist only so long as the fuel actually stored in the muscles lasts, approximately 4 seconds at maximum effort.

Anaerobic endurance can be sub-divided as follows

- Short anaerobic – less than 25 seconds (mainly alactic)
- Medium anaerobic – 25 seconds to 60 seconds (mainly lactic)
- Long anaerobic – 60 seconds to 120 seconds (lactic + aerobic)

Using repetition methods of relatively high intensity work with limited recovery can develop anaerobic endurance.

Speed Endurance

Speed endurance is used to develop the co-ordination of muscle contraction in the climate of endurance. Repetition methods are used with a high number of sets, low number of repetitions per set and intensity greater than 85% with distances covered from 60% to 120% of racing distance. Competition and time trails can be used in **the development of speed endurance.**

Strength Endurance

Strength endurance is used to develop the athlete's capacity to maintain the quality of their muscles contractile force in a climate of endurance. All athletes need to develop a basic level of strength endurance. Examples of activities to develop strength endurance are weight training, circuit training, Fartlek, hill running etc.

STRENGTH

The common definition is the ability to exert a force against a resistance. The strength needed for a sprinter to explode from the blocks is different from the strength needed by a weight lifter to lift a 200kg barbell. This, therefore, implies that there are different types of strength.

Types of Strength

- Maximum strength – the greatest force that is possible in a single maximum contraction

- Explosive strength – the ability to overcome a resistance with a fast contraction

- Strength endurance – the ability to express force many times over How do muscles get strong?

A muscle will only strengthen, when it is worked beyond its normal operation, or it is overloaded. Overload can be progressed by increasing the;

- Number of repetitions of an exercise

- Number of sets of the exercise
- Intensity – reduced recover time

Development of Strength:

- Maximum strength can be developed with
- Weight training

Explosive strength can be developed with:

- Conditioning exercises
- Medicine ball exercises
- Polymeric exercises
- Weight training

Strength endurance can be developed with:

- Circuit training
- Dumbbell exercise
- Weight training
- Hill running

SPEED

Speed is the quickness of movement of limb, whether this is the legs of a runner or the arm of the shot putter. Speed is an integral part of every sport and can be expressed as any one of, or combination of, the following

- **Maximum speed**
- **Explosive strength (power)**
- **Speed endurance**

Speed is influenced by the athlete's mobility, special strength, strength endurance and technique.

Energy system for Speed

The anaerobic a lactic pathway supplies energy for absolute

speed. The anaerobic (without oxygen) a lactic (without lactate) energy system is best challenged as an athlete approaches top speed between 30 and 60 while running at 95% to 100% of maximum. This speed component of anaerobic metabolism lasts for approximately six seconds and should be trained when no muscle fatigue is present (usually after 24 to 36 hours of rest).

Development of Speed

The technique of sprinting must be rehearsed at slow speeds and then transferred to run at maximum speed. The stimulation, excitation and correct firing order of the motor units, composed of a motor nerve (Neuron) and the group of muscles that it supplies, makes it possible high frequency movements of occur. The whole process is not totally clear but the complex coordination and timing of the motor units and muscles most certainly must be rehearsed at high speeds to implant the correct patterns.

Flexibility and a correct warm up will affect stride length and frequency. Stride length can be improved by developing muscular strength, power, strength Endurance and running technique. The development of speed is highly specific and to achieve it we should ensure that:
- Flexibility is developed and maintained all years round.
- Strength and speed is developed in parallel.
- Skill development (technique) is pre-learned, rehearsed and perfected before it is done at high-speed levels.

Speed training is developed by using high velocity for brief intervals. This will ultimately bring into play the correct neuromuscular pathways and energy sources used.

Flexibility

Flexibility is the ability to perform a joint through a range of movement. In any movement there are two groups of muscles at work:

1) Photo genetic muscles which cause the movement to take place.

2) Opposing the movement and determining the amount of flexibility are the antagonistic muscles. Flexibility training.

The objective of flexibility training is to improve the range of stretch of the antagonistic muscles.

Benefits of flexibility

Flexibility plays an important part in the preparation of athletes by developing a range of movement to allow technical development and assisting in the prevention of injury.

Flexibility exercises

The various techniques of stretching may be grouped as static, ballistic and assisted. In both static and ballistic exercises, the athlete is in control of the movements. In Assisted the movement is controlled by an external force that is usually a partner.

Static stretching

Static stretching involves gradually easing into the stretch position and holding the position. The amount of time a static stretch is held may be anything from 6 seconds to 2 minutes. Often in static stretching you are advising to move further into the stretch position as the stretch sensation subsides.

Ballistic stretching

Ballistic stretching involves some of rapid movement into the required stretch position. Where the event requires a ballistic movement, it is appropriate and perhaps necessary to conduct ballistic stretching exercise. Start off with the movement at half speed for a couple of repetitions and when gradually work up to full speed. Appropriate preparatory static stretching exercises should be conducted before any ballistic exercises are carried out.

Assisted stretching:

Assisted stretching involves the assistance of a partner who must fully understand what his role is otherwise the risk of injury is high. A partner can be employed to assist with partner stretches.

Partner stretches

Your partner assists you maintain the stretch position or help you ease into the stretch position as the sensation of stretches are best used as developmental exercises, with each stretch being held for thirty seconds.

Methods

Static methods produce far fewer instances of muscle soreness, injury and damage to connective tissues than ballistic method. Static methods are simple to carry out and may be conducted virtually anywhere. For maximum gains in flexibility in the shortest possible time ballistic stretches technique is the most appropriate. Where the technique requires ballistic movement, ballistic stretches should be employed.

When conducting flexibility exercises it is recommended to perform them in the following order static, assisted and then dynamic.

Flexibility exercises could be part of:

- The warm up program
- A standalone unit of work

It is considered beneficial to conduct flexibility exercises as part of the warm down program but should not include ballistic exercises, as the muscles are fatigued and more prone to injury.

1.4 OLYMPIC GAMES - ORIGIN AND DEVELOPMENT OF MODERN OLYMPIC GAMES. OBJECTIVES OF MODERN OLYMPIC GAMES

When we talk about Olympic games, we mean participation in international sports competitions. Participation in Sports helps people to know one another. It provides opportunities to the participants to see others. It unites countries and continents. The Olympic movement, like sport in general, by its very nature opposes the division of the world and promotes rapprochement and friendship among peoples of all continents. Neither distances nor differences in beliefs must or can prevent mankind from barring the way to the forces of insanity and war. Peace is dear and necessary to all of us. Saving it from the flames of war is every body's moral and sacred duty. Sport participation is very effective vehicle to reach and realize the said goals for the betterment of human beings of the nations.

Modern Olympic Games (From 1896 AD onwards)

For nearly 1500 years since 394 A.D. there were no Olympics. The first efforts towards renaissance of the Olympics in modern times were made by the Greek in 1859 and 1870. The Greeks and Evangelos Zappas a Greek living in Rumania, began working towards the revival of the Olympics long before Coubertin the Frenchman succeeded. Two Olympic games organsied by the Greeks in 1859 and 1870 were unsuccessful in 1894 A.D.

Baron Pierre De Coubertin a Frechman revived the Olympic games. He felt that international unity and brotherhood can be achieved through competitions in sport and games among the youth of the various countries at one place similar to the ancient Olympic Games. He visited various countries and put forth his ideas. His ideas were welcomed and it was decided to hold the first Olympics in Greece. As the ancient site at Olympia was not suitable to conduct the games. Athens in Greece was selected.

The sponsors of the Modern Olympics were hard pressed for

money. The Greek Government gave about 2 ½ lakhs of drachmae in addition to the money bequeathed by Zappas. Even this amount was not enough. Fortunately, one George Aver off a merchant of Alexandria gave a princely gift of million drachmae for restoring the Pan Athenian stadium and conducting the games.

Modern Olympics is held once in four years but during the times of world wars, the Olympic games (i.e VI, XII and XIII Olympiads respectively in the years 1916, 1940 and 1944) were and held in the days of Ancient Olympics such sanctity was attached to the games that wars were stopped for the conduct of the Olympics whereas in the days of Modern Olympics. We have witnessed that Olympic Games had to be stopped for the conduct of the wars.

Governing Body

- The international Olympic Committee is the controlling body for the Modern Olympic Games.

- The I.O.C. is a permanent and self-elected body which has at least one member from a country where there is a National Olympic committee.

- The members shall elect a president for eight years and he is eligible for reelection

- Two Vice presidents shall also be elected for a period of four years who are also eligible for re-election.

- A small Executive board shall be formed which shall include the president the two Vice presidents and four other members elected for a period of 4 years who shall retire by rotation.

- The I.O.C fixes the venue for competition draws the rules for competition draws the rules for competition and the general programme for Olympics.

Rules of Eligibility of Competition

➢ One who is a native or naturalized subject of a member country can alone participate.

➢ One who has competed already in the Olympic games for a nation cannot compete in future Olympic games for another nation even if he has become a naturalized subject of that nation except in the case of conquest or the creation of a new state ratified by a treaty.

➢ Every competitor must be an amateur This must be certified by the national body controlled that activity and countersigned by the National Olympic committee.

➢ In addition, each competitor must give a personal declaration that he is an amateur.

➢ There is no age limit for a competitor.

Organization and conduct of the Games

The Olympic Games should be held in the first years of the Olympiad. The games under no pretext can be adjourned to another year. The period of the games shall not exceed 16 days

Venue

The venue for the Olympic competitions will be fixed by a majority of votes among the members of the international Olympic committee, taking into consideration the claims made by the cities opting to stage the games. Committee from the I.O.C and the respective NOC's

(National Olympic Committees) along with the respective international sports federations visits the cities aspiring to hold the games to determine its suitability.

After various committees submit their respective reports to the IOC it takes the final decision through a ballot at a session held in a country, no city of which was a candidate. The selection unless in exceptional circumstances, is made at least six years in advances.

When the venue is fixed the mayor of that city will be informed about the decision of IOC. The Mayor in turn will inform the National Olympic Committee and this committee will take up the responsibility of Organizing and conducting the games.

Events

The events are fixed by the organizing committee in consultation with international Olympic Committee. The usual events are track and field sports, Gymnastics, Boxing, Fencing Wresting Shooting, Rowing Swimming and Diving Equestrian Sports (Horse riding) Football, water polo, Hockey, Cycling, Weightlifting yachting (Sailing, Ship racing) Basketball, Volleyball etc.

Olympic -Opening Ceremony

For opening of the games, usually the President, King or any other head of the State will be asked to preside and declare the games open. The president will then mount up the Tribune of Honour and the National Anthem of the host country will be played.

The march past of the athletes and the officials will take place according to the alphabetical order of the countries. In the march past the Greek contingent will always take the lead while the host country will be at the end.

The president of the games will declare open the Olympiad of the modern era Hoisting of the Olympic flag with fanfare of trumpets followed by a salute of gun fire and pigeons release.

The Olympic torch will be brought into the stadium and the Olympic flames will be lit in the bowl constructed for this purpose. The flames will be burning throughout the period of the Olympic Games.

All the bearers will move forward to the Rostrum and stand in a semicircular fashion facing the Tribune of Honour.

The Olympic oath will be taken by a representative of the athletes usually an athlete of the host country who will take the following oath.

The Olympic oath will be taken by a representative of the athletes usually an athlete of the host country who will take the following oath.

We swear that we will take part in the Olympic games in loyal competition respecting the regulations which govern them and desirous of participating in them in the true spirit of sportsmanship for the honour of our country and for the glory of sports.

Presently this oath has been revised a sunder and given effect from Sydney Olympics 2002.

In the name of all competitors I promise that we shall take part in this Olympic game respecting and abiding by the rules which govern them without the use of doping and drugs in the true spirit of sportsmanship for the glory of sports and the honour of our teams.

After the Oath the National Anthem of the host country will be played. The athletes and the Officials shall march out of the stadium. The games shall then begin.

Awards

Those who get the first three places will mount the Victory stand. The first place winner will be at the centre at a higher level.

The second place winners will be on his right and the third place winners on his left. As soon as they have mounted the victory stand the national flags of the winners will go up the masts. The National Anthem of the winner will be briefly played.

The victors will be crowned with Olive Wreaths. The President of the International Olympic committee or his representatives will give away medals and diplomas (Gold Medal for I place, Silver Medal for II place and Bronze medal for III place)

The banes of the victors will be inscribed on the walls of the stadium where the Olympics games are conducted. In addition a Roll of honour is keep with the international Olympic Committee in which the names of the first six competitions are entered. Competitors who have secured IV, V and VI places in each event are awarded only Diplomas. Souvenir medals are given to all participants.

Closing of the Games

The closing of the games will take place in a solemn manner. The president of the International Olympic Committee will express his gratitude to the organizers. He will then declare the games closed and will call upon the youth of the various countries to assemble again after four years at the next venue of the games.

Immediately after his declaration the ceremonial Olympic flag (not the one that was hoisted on the flag mast) will be handed over to the Mayor of the city, so that he can keep the flag safety till the next Olympic Games. Then trumpets will be sounded, the Olympic flames will be extinguished and the Olympic flag will be lowered. Thus the games come to a close.

Olympic Flag

There are two kinds of flags used by the International Olympics Committee

1. Olympic flag for hoisting purpose during Olympic

Ceremonial Olympic flag

Olympic flag

This Olympic flag is based on a model design by Braon de

Coubertin in 1914 It was first hoisted in 1920 at Antwerp (Beigium) Olympics

The Olympic flag is made of white silk without any borders. In the centre, there are five interacted rings in the colours of Blue, Yellow, Black, Green and Red representing the five continents viz. America, Asia, Africa, Europe and Australia.

> The five rings are arranged in the shape of a W

> The blue ring shall be high on the left nearer the flag pole.

Below the rings appears the Olympic Motto **Citius Altius Fortius** which means ever faster, higher, stronger.

Those rings together with the motto constitute the Olympic emblem which is the exclusive properly of the International Olympic committee.

Only the flag is hoisted during the Olympic Games

(ii) Ceremonial Olympic flag

This flag is made of silk and this is borded with the colours of the rings (blue , yellow, black, green and red)

This flag is not intended for hoisting purpose

The flag is handed over to the Mayor of the city conducting the concerned Olympics by the president of I.O.C at the time of the closing ceremony. This shall be under the custody of the Mayor of the city till the next Olympics

Motto of the modern Olympic games

The Olympic Games had come to stay in 1897. The international Olympic games committee adopted a Dominican monks worlds. Citius Aitius, Fortius Ever (fastest, highest, strongest) as the Olympic motto to embody the spirit of the games.

The most important thing in the game is not to win but to take part just as the most important thing in life is not the triumph but the struggle. The essential thing is not to have conquered but to have fought well.

Olympic Torch

The ritual flame lighting ceremony takes place at the temples of Hera, near the stadium where the ancient Olympics were held. An actress from the Greek national theatre, portraying a priest-ess , uses a concave mirror to catch the sun's rays to ignite the torch which is then handed over to young athletes who carry it for one kilometer each (if it has to be flown, the flame is kept in specially made lanterns while it is being transported to the hot nation).

This torch shall then be relayed on foot (as for as possible) by runners until it is finally taken to the city where the games are to be conducted.

On its way as it passes through various countries the particular country through which it passes shall arrange for the relay of runners to bear the torch. The last runners shall be an athlete from the host country and his arrival with the torch will be synchronized with the opening of the games.

This was first initiated by the Germans while they organsied the Berlin Olympic Games in the year 1936. From bertin Olympic onwards this practice is continued. Now a day's torch is also carried in aero planes from one country to another where it is not possible to carry it by a relay of runners.

UNIT - 2

II CONCEPT OF HEALTH EDUCATION

2.1 Meaning, Definition, Aims, Objectives and Importance of Health Education.

2.2 Communicable and Non-Communicable Diseases.

2.3 First-Aid- Principles of First Aid, Concept of First Aid Box, Reasons of Sports Injuries.

2.4 Healthful school Environment. Medical inspection

2.1 MEANING, DEFINITION, AIMS, OBJECTIVES AND IMPORTANCE OF HEALTH EDUCATION.

Health is a very important topic and so is health education. Healthy people constitute a healthy nation. It is necessary to explain the meaning of health as it is not merely absence of disease but much more. In this chapter apart from elaborating the meanings of health and health education, definitions of health and health education, and various dimensions of health, the objectives, the scope, principles and importance of health education have also been discussed.

Meaning of Health

The strength of a nation rests upon the health of its people and future of the health of the people depends, to a large extent, on what is done to promote, improve and preserve the health, as health is a fundamental human right. To be a good man is the first requisite to succeed in life and to be a nation of healthy citizens is the first condition to national prosperity. The natural question that arises is, what health is ? and on what it depends ?

The dictionary meaning of health is, **Freedom from disease, sound body and mind and mind are duly discharged"**. Earlier, health was considered as a condition of being hale', i.e. safe and sound. A more searching and deep look in the subject would show that health is more than this. The implication of health is that, health may be a continuum along linear scale, from near death at one end to optimum health of the other. Opitrnum health would be that level which would enable the individual to live life to the fullest. Health is the ability of the body to sustain adaptive efforts and is used to imply body power, vitality, and ability to resist fatigue. Health is sometimes considered as the total outcome of the organic, neuro- muscular, interpretive, and emotional development.

Health is man's greatest wealth, he who has health must cherish it with care, lest he should lose it. To this end he must have adequate knowledge of how to live healthy. Health is not merely absence of disease, it is positive quality of the living body, of which fitness for one's work and happiness are distinguishing marks.

Definition of Health

Recently this definition has been amplified and it has been added, "attainment of a level of health that will enable every individual to lead a socially and economically productive life. " -**World Health Organisation**

"Health means soundness of body or mind;that condition in which its functions are dulyand efficiently discharged." -**Oxford English Dictionary.**

"Health is a state of complete physical, mental and social wellbeing and not merely an absence of diseases or infirmity."

"Health is the condition of being sound in body, mind or spirit, especially freedom from physical disease or pain." -**Webster**

"Health is considered as that condition, mental and physical, in which the individual is functionally well adjusted internally as concerns his body parts, and externally as concerns his environments." -**Voltmer and Esslinger**

"One's ideal of health should be the highest realisation of his physical, mental and spiritual possibilities rather than mere freedom from diseases and deformities." **-W.A. Yeager**

"It is the quality of life that enables an individual to live most and serve best." **- J.F. Williams**

"Health is a state of relative equilibrium of body form and function which results from its successful dynamic adjustment to forces tending to disturb it. It is not passive interplay between body substance and forces impinging upon it but an active response of body forces working towards readjustment." -**Perkins**

Meaning of Health Education

Health education is rather an abstract term, meaning different things to different people. To some, it is a matter of public relations stating the activities of health department, and to many others it provides knowledge about health and diseases.

Anything that educates anyone in the matter of health, is health education, i.e. the education given for identifying the health needs and matching it with suitable adaptive behavior, can be termed as health education. In simple words, the entire process of involving people in learning about health and disease, making efforts for improving health and facilitating them to act appropriately for overcoming ailments and promoting a positive health, is health education.

"Health education, like general education, is concerned with changes in knowledge, feelings and behavior of people. In its most usual forms, it concentrates on developing such health practices as are believed to bring about the best possible state of well- being."-**W.H.0. Technical Report (1954)**

It is apparent from this definition that health education is a process that helps people to find out their health needs, activates them for adopting suitable behavior and building up right attitude for achieving and maintaining optimum health. Health education brings about changes in the knowledge and attitude of people and thereby affects the changes in their health practices. It is concerned with establishing changes in personal and group attitudes and behavior that promote healthier living. The object of health education is to win friends and influence people", and it is an essential tool of community health.

Briefly it is stated, that health education recognises three basic components

a) Unity of human beings in respect to their physical, mental, and social aspect.

b) The knowledge, attitudes, and practices are important to influence health behavior.

c) The focus of health education on the individual, family and community.

All these components of health education are inter-dependent and constantly interact with each other.

Health educationists have recognised the importance of instilling, in young and old alike, a body of health knowledge based on scientific facts, wholesome health attitude and desirable health practices. The art and science of engaging people in the process of learning, for the desired behavior, for the preservation of health, is health education.

Definitions of Health Education

"Health Education aims at creating such a quality of life as may enable an individual to live most and to serve best. " -**W.H.O.**

"Health Education is concerned with the health related behavior of people." -**Sophie**

"Anything that educates anyone in the matter of health, is health education. It is concerned with the knowledge of all round healthy habits –**Thomas Wood.'"**

"Health education is a process that bridges the gap between health information and health practices. Health Education motivates the person to take the information and do something with it, to keep himself healthier, by avoiding actions that are harmful, and practicing those that are beneficial." -**President's Committee on health Education, New York.**

"Health Education is the sum of all those experiences in school, and elsewhere, that favorably influence habits, attitudes and knowledge related to individual, community and social health." -**Thomnas Wood**

"Health education is the translation of what is known about health into desirable individual and community behavior patterns by means of the educational process. -**Ruth. E. Grout**

"Health education, like general education, is concerned with changes in knowledge, feelings and behavior of people. In its most usual forms it concentrates on developing such health practices as are believed to bring about the best possible state of wellbeing."-**W.H.0. Technical Report (1954)**

"Health education is a process that informs, motivates, and helps people to adopt and maintain healthy practices and life styles, advocates environmental changes, as needed, to facilitate this goal, and conducts professional training and research to the same end. **"-Anne R. Somers**

Objectives of Health Education

After analysing the definition of health education as given by Somers and adopted by National Conference on Preventive Medicine (U.S.A.), J.E. Park stated three main objectives of health education.

   a.   Informing people.
   b.   Motivating people.
   c.   Guiding into action.

Some other authors have also suggested similar objectives, however, naming the same differently i.e.

   a.   Development of health knowledge.
   b.   Development of desirable health attitude.
   c.   Development of desirable health practices.

In order to overcome any confusion or ambiguity, if any, in the minds of readers/students with regard to the above stated twin sets of objectives, having been clubbed, as given below:

1. **Informing People/Development of Health Knowledge:**

The first objective of health education is to inform people or to develop health knowledge by presenting and interpreting scientific health data based on research and discoveries. Such information will help the individuals to recognise health problems and to solve them by utilising this valid information. It will also help in removing ignorance, prejudice, blind believes and misconceptions regarding health and hygiene.

2. **Motivating People/Development of Desirable / Health Attitude:**

Merely informing people about health is not enough. They must be motivated to the point that they want to apply this knowledge to everyday living by favorably changing their behavior patterns, their attitudes, their habits and ways of living. Individuals acquiring such healthy attitudes will! tend to transmit this knowledge to their families, community, society and nation, for healthful living.

3. Guiding into Action / Development of Desirable Health Practices:

Knowledge will be of little use unless it ensures good health and strains of daily life. Similarly, an practices and guides people to adopt and maintain healthy life styles. The health practices will determine, to a great extent, the health status of the person. Adopting harmful habits or practices will result in poor health whereas beneficial health habits will result in good and positive health.

To sum up, knowledge without incentive or motivation will not ensure desirable health attitudes and health practices. Thus these three objectives have close relationship and contribute to each other.

Ruth. E. Grout has stated four objectives of health education :

- Optimum development of the individual with special reference to physical and emotional development.

- Betterment of human relationships, particularly from the and point of health.

- Application of health facts and principles in respect of economic efficiency in the production and consumption of goods and services.

- Civic responsibility, especially in respect to health.

These objectives are discussed as under:

a. Opitmum Development of the Individual with Special Reference to Physical and Emotional Development:

Optimum development of an individual refers to the development of all the aspects of his personality. It is that state in which the individual is able to utilise and mobilize all his resources to lead an optimum and meaningful life. An individual, who is physically fit and emotionally stable, tends to lead a healthy life.

By engaging in physical activities apart from physical fitness, one is able to achieve maximum satisfaction in everyday life, better neuro-muscular coordination, better mental emotionally stable person is able to control his emotions and channelise his energies in a positive direction. For the development of the healthy personality, emotional stability and wholesome emotional expression is essential Physically developed person will tend to be emotionally satisfied and will accept challenges. These two aspects are just like two sides of a coin, each supplement and compliment one another.

b. Betterment of Human Relationship, Particularly from the Stand Point of Health:

Human relationship is a key to happiness and a expected to have good relations with his fellow beings. The objective of health education is the establishment and improvement of human relations through positive interaction between human beings, within family, and community at large. Health education contributes to the betterment of human relationships in many ways. A healthy person can easily identify himself with the group, he can think for betterment and welfare of the others, and tries to co-operate and coordinate with others. Such a person is better adjusted in family, community and society, thus promoting much better human relationships.

c. Application of Health Facts and principles in Respect of economic Efficacy in Production and Consumption of Goods and Services:

Each individual has to adopt some vocation profession in vocation, profession or trade, and has to be economic efficiency, be it in production and has to be regulated and controlled by applying consumption of goods or in providing services, facts and principles of health, as any depart health. Production and consumption has to be from the same might jeopardize the national done in healthy and hygienic conditions. The basic facts and principles of health are not to remain confined to an individual's own personality but have to be reflected in the production and consumption of goods and services provided to the society, to ensure good health of the society. It is an objective of health education to educate the people on this important issue.

d. Civic Responsibility, Especially in Respect to Health:

Another objective of health education is to contribute in cultivating a sense of civic responsibility in individuals. Health education aims to develop an individual in all aspects so as to produce a healthy, law abiding and useful citizens who possess all the civic qualities like co-operation, love, service to others, fellowship, sacrifice, sense of duty, sense of responsibility etc. Health education, through its service programmes, provides exposure to the individuals enabling them to Imbibe a sense of duty, to spread the message of health. Such a healthy citizen can effectively play his role in the development of a healthy Society as well as in the development of a healthy nation.

Importance of Health Education

Knowledge of health education assumes great importance in India, where most of the people are ignorant about the basic principles of health and hygiene. Because of this ignorance, they are unable to prevent the diseases, most of which are preventable. There is an emergent need to remove this ignorance of masses. They are to be made aware of fundamental and basic principles of health and hygiene. Health education provides the scientific facts of community hygiene that could help in preventing and eradicating many diseases and remove ignorance. Health education programmes are basically of preventive and promotive nature. As prevention is better than cure, such programmes are very important in transmitting the knowledge, making the people aware of various dreaded diseases, occurrence of which could be easily avoided. In this way, health education can play an important role in eliminating many problems that adversely affect young people, adults, and society in general.

It is necessary for a prosperous country to have healthy citizens. Health education has a very significant role to play as it comprises health knowledge, health habits and health attitudes. It can improve the individual, family and community life for a bright and prosperous future.

Health education helps an individual to distinguish between good and bad health habits and encourages him to make good habits as enduring and lasting healthful behavior. Health education is essential to assure that proper health habits are established early in life, as habits and behavior adopted in childhood remain unchanged even in adult life. The good health habits instilled in children during their formative years reflect in their life, making them healthy, useful, and effective citizen of the country. In this way health education also contributes to national growth.

Health Education is a comprehensive, qualitative and a dynamic process of education as:

- It develops sound attitudes towards the importance of good health and safety practice at home and in the community.

- It provides direct learning experience to encourage the practice of wholesome healthy habits in daily living.

- It introduces students to the areas of health knowledge, enabling them to better understand and cope-up with individual and community health problems.

- It introduces students to the basic mechanism and functions of human body.

- It integrates the many sources of health information in the biological, social and physical sciences so that they can be applied in a meaningful way towards establishing a total health concept.

- It helps students to achieve deeper insight into the nature of social relationships and family life.

- It furnishes a setting for learning which enables the students to realize their fullest potentialities.

- It encourages the development of responsibility and cooperation among students in observing environmental controls.

- It contributes to the education of physically challenged people, enabling them to make the most of educational opportunities available.

Health education has become increasingly important in the recent years due to the attention given by the printed and electronic media with regard to the general concern about social-medical problems. Nowadays health is considered as a worldwide social goal. Health education is of great importance as its main aim is to achieve optimum health of an individual which include all the dimensions of heath i.e.

physical, mental social emotional and spiritual. Health education has become one of the most important disciplines of education. Health education is basic to learning, to happiness, to success, to effective citizenship and to worthwhile living.

2.2 COMMUNICABLE AND NON-COMMUNICABLE DISEASES

A disease is any abnormal condition that obstructs normal bodily functions and often leads to a feeling of pain and weakness. It is usually associated with symptoms and signs. It is a pathologic condition in which the normal functioning of the body is impaired or disrupted, resulting in distress, or death. We can say that good health is the state where we are physically, mentally, and socially fit, and disease is a factor that affects health. A condition can be either due to structural disorder or functional abnormality in the body.

Infectious diseases, deficiency diseases, hereditary diseases (including genetic and non-genetic hereditary disorders), and physiological diseases are the four basic categories of diseases. Diseases can also be divided into categories such as communicable and non-communicable. Here, we will talk about communicable diseases and non-communicable diseases.

We can call diseases those abnormalities in our body, which cause discomfort as a result of organs or organ systems being affected. It is essential to know that there is a condition that is responsible for the improper functioning of the body. We realize that something is wrong when we notice the signs and symptoms. A proper diagnosis of the disease is possible by visible signs that our body exhibits. These signs are called symptoms. It is these symptoms that help in the accurate diagnosis of the disease. The study of disease is called pathology.

Communicable Diseases

The term "communicable disease" refers to illnesses that can be passed from one person to another through a variety of means. The spread of communicable diseases is aided and accelerated by socioeconomic, environmental, and behavioral variables, as well as international travel and migration. It includes contact with blood and bodily fluids, breathing an airborne virus, or by an insect bite.

Vaccine-preventable, foodborne, zoonotic, healthcare-related, and communicable diseases are all serious hazards to human health, and they can even jeopardize global health security. The pathogen or infectious agent, as well as the mode of transmission, determine how these diseases spread.

Examples of Communicable Diseases:

1. AIDS
2. Polio
3. Measles
4. Influenza
5. Tuberculosis
6. Whooping cough
7. Typhoid
8. Cholera

Causes

Pathogens that are transferred from one organism to another produce communicable diseases. Pathogens are organisms that cause disease. Viruses, bacteria, fungus, protozoa, and worms are the five basic forms of pathogenic organisms.

Symptoms

Communicable diseases commonly cause headaches, runny noses, flu, vomiting, fever, dysentery, diarrhea, cough, malaria, muscle aches, rabies, itching, and other symptoms.

Treatment

- ➤ The treatment of the communicable disease depends on the type of microorganism that causes the infection.

- ➤ If bacteria create a disease, antibiotic treatment usually kills the bacteria and brings the infection to a close.

- ➤ Supportive therapy, such as rest and increased hydration intake, are frequently used to treat viral infections.

- ➤ Antifungal and antiparasitic treatments, such as fluconazole, and antiparasitic pharmaceuticals, such as mebendazole, are used to treat fungal and parasitic infections.

Non-Communicable Diseases

Non-communicable diseases or NCDs generally are long-lasting and progress slowly, and thus they are sometimes also referred to as chronic diseases. They can also result from exposure to adverse environments or from genetically determined abnormalities, which may be seen at birth or which may become apparent later in life. The majority of non-communicable infectious diseases are non-infectious, except parasitic disorders where the parasite's life cycle does not require direct host-to-host transmission.

Examples of Major Non–Communicable Disease Include:
1. Parkinson's disease
2. Autoimmune diseases
3. Strokes
4. The majority of heart diseases
5. The majority of cancers
6. Diabetes
7. Chronic kidney disease
8. Osteoarthritis
9. Osteoporosis
10. Alzheimer's disease
11. Cataracts,

Causes

Non-communicable diseases (NCDs) are referred to as "lifestyle" diseases because the majority of these illnesses are preventable. Tobacco use (smoking), hazardous alcohol use, poor diets (high consumption of sugar, salt, saturated fats, and trans-fatty acids), and physical inactivity are the most common causes.

Symptoms

- ➢ Short of breath
- ➢ Severe pain or discomfort in the chest
- ➢ Rapid and irregular heartbeat
- ➢ Dizziness and weakness
- ➢ Severe headache
- ➢ Confusion, difficulty speaking or understanding speech
- ➢ Loss of strength in arms and legs
- ➢ Dropping face, arm, leg especially on one side of the body
- ➢ Difficulty of seeing with one or both eyes
- ➢ Fainting or unconsciousness

Treatment

There is no permanent cure for NCDs. Medications and therapies help in relieving most of the symptoms. NCDs are lifestyle diseases. Prevention and management are better than cure in case of NCDs. In the case of cancer, early diagnosis helps in treatment. Lifestyle changes such as giving up on smoking and alcohol can bring about improvements in the case of NCDs.

2.3 FIRST-AID- PRINCIPLES OF FIRST AID, CONCEPT OF FIRST AID BOX, REASONS OF SPORTS INJURIES.

What men call accident is the doing of God's providence". Accidents often take place at home, in schools, on play fields, industries or elsewhere. So everyone should know what to do in such situation. If proper help is not given in time the patient's condition could get worse or if proper care is not taken it may cause danger to life. The need and importance of first aid is more realized when any individual dies before you just due to the poor knowledge or ignorance of first aid.

Physical Education and Sports activities demand sufficient knowledge of first aid since participation in sports involves variety oi movements which some time lead to variety of injuries. Therefore, whosoever enters in the play field, Gymnasium, swimming pool, different kinds of terrain and so on must have the knowledge of fundamental principles of first aid. He may be a teacher, trainer, trainee, attendant on the swimming pool and in the gymnasium. Injury in sports may be as small as minor scratch on the body and as serious as may be danger to the life, needing prompt first aid. First aid needs to be immediate in severe First-Aid accidents complicated by bleeding, shock and loss of consciousness.

Meaning and Definitions of First Aid

The terms First Aid' was adopted officially in England for the first time in 1879 by the St. John Ambulance Association. First aid is a combination of simple but quite effective and active measures to prevent possible complications. First Aid means the treatment given to the casualty till proper medical aid comes. In other words, the first aid is the process of carrying out the essential emergency treatment of an injury/illness in order to benefit the casualty till the proper medical services are rendered.

First aid is the immediate and temporary care given to the victim of an accident or sudden illness. Purpose of First Aid is an immediate care till the medical aid is given by the competent and qualified medical personnel.

Purpose of First Aid

The purpose of First Aid' is to preserve life, assist recovery and prevent aggravation of the of the condition, until the services of a doctor can be obtained, or during transport to hospital or to the casualty's home.

The First Aider

The term or expression First Aider" was not coined till 1894 and was intended to designate any person who has received a certificate from an authorised association that he or she is qualified to render First Aid.

The Prerequisite Personal Qualities of First Aider

The following are some of the utmost important personal qualities of the First Aider" :

1. He should be calm and quite.
2. He should be able to maintain order as far as possible until the arrival of or reaching at emergency center, where emergency staff assume control.
3. He should be quick but not hasty in taking decisions.
4. He should be observant about conditions arising out of accident.
5. He should be tactful and polite in order to take help from people around for calling doctor, arranging ambulance / transport for shifting to a hospital or informing at the nearby police station.
6. He should be innovative to use some other first aid material instead of real one, if need arises.

Types of First Aid

There are two types of First Aid":

• *Self Aid*
• *First Aid*

Self-Aid, is what injured person (casualty) can do for himself. In many cases the first form of help/aid is provided by the affected person himself. Much can usefully be done by the casualty himself in stopping bleeding, supporting injured parts, covering the wounds, summoning others for help and reaching the nearby health center for emergency treatment, if possible.

First Aid, means what other people can do for the casualty when he / she is unconscious or unable to move; there help provided to the casualty is known First Aid. He may be a person trained for the purpose or at least knowing the underlying principles of the First Aid. He can give skilled help, prevent death, promote recovery and see that an injury or condition of casualty does not get worse until the doctor arrives.

Principles of First Aid

1. Do first things first quickly, quietly, and without panic.
2. Guard against or treat for shock by moving the casualty as little as possible and handling him gently.
3. Do not attempt too much.
4. Reassure the casualty and those around in order to reduce tension.
5. Give artificial respiration, if breathing has stopped.
6. Stop any bleeding.
7. Do not allow people to crowd around as fresh air is essential.
8. Do not remove clothes unnecessarily.
9. Arrange for the removal of the casualty to the care of a doctor or hospital as soon as possible.

Functions of The First Alder

In order to control the emergency situation, reaching at the place of casualty, the first aider should obtain a brief history of accident/cause of injury from the patient or from people around, if the patient is unconscious.

The following functions should be considered utmost important to identify the emergency priorities:

1. **General condition of the patient :** Assess the general condition of the patient in terms of nature of injury (serious/minor), age, physical status (disabled/not), conscious or unconscious, fracture or dislocation, and so on.

2. **Pulse of the patient :** If the pulse is weak and rapid it indicates severe bleeding. If the pulse is not felt, it indicates cardiac arrest/ heart attack.

3. **Respiration :** Check the breathing rhythm of the casualty, whether it is normal, slow, or fast. When the patient cannot breathe, artificial respiration should be carried out at once and this is continued till the revival of re- operation/arrival of proper medical aid. Clothing around the chest and the neck is loosened.

4. **Colour of tongue, lips, conjunctiva (eyes) and nails:** If the colour of tongue or lips is blue it indicates lack of oxygen. Whiteness (Pallor) of the tongue, eyes (conjunctiva) and nails indicates severity of bleeding.

5. **Bleeding :** Parts of the body particularly the ears, mouth, nose and limbs for fracture must be checked for bleeding.

6. Burns : In case of burns, the cause, degree and site of the burn should be noted.

7. **Fracture of a bone or dislocation of a joint :** Limbs/joints of the body should be examined carefully to see if there is any fracture / dislocation of a joint, accordingly first Aid arrangements may be made.

8. **Poisoning :** In suspected cases of poisoning, signs and symptoms should be observed carefully. The vomiting material may be collected if possible for the identification of poison.

First Aid Box

This is a small and handy kit box which contains the following articles required by the First Aider while providing First Aid :

1. Sterile gauge pieces.
2. Bandages of different sizes.
3. Adhesive plasters of different sizes.
4. Scissors, safety pins, needles, tweezers etc.
5. Pads of various sizes.
6. Splints
7. Antiseptics, e.g., Dettol, spirit, tincture and so on.
8. Silver sulfa diazine cream.
9. Drugs e.g., analgesics, antibiotics, packets of O.R.S. etc.

The complete first aid box should be readily available in every home, institution, houses, factories, public places, swimming pools, gymnasium halls, and play fields for immediate use.

Reasons of Sports Injuries

Injuries on the play fields, swimming pool and gymnasium may take place due to the reasons listed below:

1. Poor physical fitness of players/students.
2. Poor mental/psychological preparation to take part in a

particular activity/game.

3. Inadequate warming up before practicing/competition.

4. By using substandard sports equipment or sports wears.

5. Adopting faulty skill of the particular game.

6. Lack of knowledge of rules of the game/s.

7. Poor maintenance of sports fields/surfaces of gymnasium /swimming pools.

8. Absence of a qualified supervisor/a coach/a teacher on sports fields.

9. Absence of a life savior/guard on the swimming pool.

10. Arrogant behavior of a player.

11. Adverse climatic for training/competition.

12. Heterogeneous grouping of physical education class or team for practice/ training.

13. Avoiding the use of sports guards.

If the above given reasons are kept in mind and looked into seriously, the chances of sports injuries are minimized to a greater extent.

2.4 HEALTHFUL SCHOOL ENVIRONMENT, MEDICAL INSPECTION

In a healthy school environment student, parents, staff, administration and community support the student wellness policy, nutrition education and school meals programs with the shared values of healthy eating, active living and sustainable environmental practices.

The core elements of a healthy school environment include access to healthcare, healthy food and physical activity, clean air and water, and education about making healthy choices. In a healthy school, students learn through lessons and by example to value their own health and that of their environment.

In a healthy school, students learn through lessons and by example-to value their own health and that of their environment. The components of a healthy school include:

1. Healthy spaces to learn and play

2. Health as an integral part of excellence in education

3. Knowledgeable teachers, administrators and staff

4. Access to physical and behavioral health services

5. Involved parents and community members

Characteristics of A Healthy School Environment and community

1. Attention to culture is everywhere. As explained by author and researcher Samuel Cásey Carter, while students do learn during class, there's also much that is learned implicitly, outside of the classroom, during a school day. A collaborative School where the mission is reflected in each interaction will take this into account.

2. A nurturing environment with high expectations Culture isn't dictated by one person, it's created by a community. Supporting and challenging individuals in a nurturing environment not only rives growth, but ensures that community members are engaged.

3. Engaged staff, engaged students -According to a 2018 Gallup poll, engaged students are 4.5 times more likely to be hopeful about the future than disengaged peers. A study from Cardwell echoes the importance of engagement, finding that students who reported high levels of teacher support indicated that they also had higher levels of engagement.

4. A commitment to lifelong learning Beliefs, values and actions spread the farthest when learning is actively happening at every level. In education, every member of the school community should feel compelled to participate in the learning process. Teachers who model inquiry, curiosity, and even uncertainty create the understanding that what students have not yet learned, can be learned. And that a desire to learn is the first and most essential Step in this process.

5. Holistic sense of responsibility -As stated in Harvard Business Review's The Culture Factor, when aligned with strategy and leadership, a strong culture drives positive Selecting Outcomes. Organizational or developing leaders for the future requires a forward-looking strategy and culture.

Effective action to create and maintain a healthful and safe school environment requires cooperation from the following:

- Teachers as advocates, including school staff members

- Students' involvement

- Parent and community Involvement

Multitude of dynamic conditions that areexternal to the person

Two types:

➢ **Supportive:** creates healthful choices or protects the well-being of the student (e.g./food service programs)
➢ **Non-supportive:** detracts from Commitment for healthful behavior (e.g Vending machines/containing junk food)

Enhancing Physical Conditions that Facilitate Optimal Learning & Development

1. School size
2. Lighting
3. Color choices
4. Temperature or Ventilation
5. Noise Control
6. Sanitation/Cleanliness
7. Other Physical Conditions
8. Accessibility

1. SCHOOL SIZE

➢ School and classroom size are important environmental conditions.

➢ Teachers and school professionals have little control over this.

➢ Student distraction is more likely in large classes Compared to smaller ones.

➢ Small schools offer greater opportunities to participate in extracurricular activities and leadership roles.

2. LIGHTING

➢ Most critical physical characteristic of the class room.

➢ Key to the well-being of students and teachers who are Confined in a class room.

➢ Poor lighting can affect students' attitudes and mood.

➢ General classroom illumination requires 50-100 foot candles.

➢ Adequate lighting promotes effective academic work, discourages unsanitary conditions, and encourages high morale.

COLOR CHOICES

➤ Color can transform a school's atmosphere from Depressing and monotonous to:

- ✓ Inviting
- ✓ Pleasing
- ✓ Stimulating

TEMPERATURE AND VENTILATION

➤ Temperatures that are too high deplete energy from students.

➤ Temperatures that are too low can make students restless inattentive.

➤ Optimal class room should range between 65-70 degrees Fahrenheit.

➤ During and/or hot make Sure students are hydrating on a regular basis.

NOISE CONTROL

➤ Noise can make it difficult for students to learn for several reasons.

➤ Noise raises stress levels for students and teachers.

➤ Classroom noise can be controlled by using noise absorbing materials.

➤ Long-term exposure can lead to hearing loss.

SANITATION ANDCLEANLINESS

➤ Sanitation is the protection of health and prevention of disease by removing filth and infectious materials.

➤ Personal hand-washing procedures should be stressed among all students and school personnel.

➤ All schools should have a standard policy promoting this important concept.

OTHER PHYSICAL CONDITIONS

Here are some possible conditions that could impact a student's well-being:

- ➢ Optimal space for physical activity
- ➢ Watch for "hidden spaces"
- ➢ Storage of chemicals
- ➢ Sun exposure
- ➢ Animals in the classrooms

ACCESSIBILITY

- ➢ Students with physical disabilities often require modifications to gain access to several facilities.

- ➢ Access often requires installation of special equipment or modifications of existing facilities.

SCHOOL SITE

School Site means a plot of ground or property set apart for the use of a school and it is the land set aside for each type of school, such as Elementary, Junior High, Senior High operated by the School Board, including but not limited to municipal school reserve.

Why is school site important in education?

Selecting and acquiring suitable school sites important part of the school plant planning process. school's site is one of the factors that can either enhance or hinder the implementation of its instructional and non- instructional programs. The site is also one of the factors that can determine how useful a school plant can be to the members if the local community. School administrators should, therefore, be concerned with the present and future needs of their school sites.

Importance of Having Healthy School Environment and School Site

They protect children's health. They enhance learning. They are pleasant places to be. Finally, safe and healthy schools are often environmentally friendly schools, which use less energy, produce fewer pollutants, and model environmental responsibility for teachers and students.

Every child deserves a healthy and safe place to learn, grow and develop. Healthy school environments support healthier children. Healthier children are less likely to be absent and more likely to achieve their academic goals.

Healthy schools can reduce energy and maintenance costs, while providing cleaner indoor air, improved lighting and reduced exposures to toxic substances. This leads to a healthier and safer learning environment for children and work environment for personnel, fostering better attendance, achievement and productivity.

Health Education in Schools

Programme of health education should not confine itself to personal hygiene of pupils only. It should include all aspects which may help in promoting health of the community as a whole. A school programme is twofold.

(i) Prevention of the development of poor health

(ii) Preservation of good health

The school health program is divided in to three parts

- Health instruction

- Health service

- Health supervision

HEALTH INSTRUCTION

The school has major responsibility in the area of health instruction. It should instruct youth in such things as the structures and functioning of their bodies the causes and methods of preventing certain diseases, the factors that contribute to and maintain good health, and the role of the community in the health program. Such an instructional program if planned wisely and taught intelligently will contribute to good health habits and attitudes on the part of the student.

Health instruction should avoid too much stress on the field of diseases and medicine. This is pointed out by Dr. Baue health authority in an article entitled Teach Health Not Disease. He says that teachers should primarily teach health how to live correctly and how to protect one's body against infection rather that teaches diseases and medicine. Proper health instruction should impress upon each individual his responsibility of his own health and as a member of a community for the health of others.

Definition

Health instruction is that organization of learning experience directed towards development of favourable health knowledge attitude and practice. – D. K. Barle

Aim

The aim of health instruction is to acquaint pupils about the functioning of the various organs of the body the rules of health and hygiene and methods for curing diseases.

Methods of imparting health instructions

There is nothing very special about the methods of imparting health Education. Health Education forma an essential part of total education. As such all aspects of health education should be carried on at all stages of the educational process according to the age and maturity. The following are some of the important ways and means through which health education and its instruction can be imparted effectively in institutions.

1. Healthful Environment of the institution

Environment is the most important of all educational media. Any scheme of health education must receive top priority to the improvement of physical and human environment. Neat clean attractive and well maintained institutional building, classrooms, equipment's and plays fields, sympathetic and affectionate teachers contribute greatly to inculcate healthful living, health habits and conditions of work and health notions about work and life. As is the environment. So is the individual therefore healthful environment of the institution plays key role in achieving success.

2. Systematic Health Instructions

Direct health instruction should be provided through subjects like hygiene, physiology, general science physical education home science social studies etc. This will enable students to understand the structures and function of human body realize the need for keeping physically fit and take precautionary and remedial measures in case of illness and diseases. Such instruction will also lay emphasis on physical exercises, sports, games and nutritional value of different kinds of food and diet.

3. Incidental Teaching

At the school stage the teacher can give health instruction in the class room situation when there is any incident of communicable disease in the school. In this way such incidental teaching may benefit the individual or the entire class. Similarly teachers have opportunities to give instruction off and on, on personal hygiene in a simple language which is benefit at for the school and community as a whole.

4. Lectures on health by experts

The school authorities should make arrangement on certain occasions to request medical officer or physical instructor and other experts on health to visits the school and to deliver a lecture on various items o health and hygiene. However emphasis should be laid on the fact that talks should be supplemented by illustrative aids and material. At the end of the talk the pupils must be given opportunities to ask any questions concerning the topic to get their doubts cleared.

5. Printed Material

The school can accumulate printed material on health and hygiene such as short leaflets, pamphlets posters and standard books. Even the school authority can have the material from the local health department to highlight certain diseases, their causes and cures.

6. Films and Film Strips

The school can arrange documentary film from various sources which generally displayed the various diseases and how to prevent ourselves from these. They also stress the importance of personal habits like cleanliness. Similarly film strips accompanied by talks or commentary by experts can be displayed and may be retained on the screen as long as wishes.

7. School broadcast and radio talks

Radio talks are a powerful medium for giving health instruction to the young pupil and reaching a wide public at the same time. Radio talks can be delivered on problem of health and hygiene by way of songs or play. In this way the children not only get entertainment but useful instruction also similarly the school broadcast programme does include items of health and hygiene.

8. Educational field trips

Actual field trips provide learning situation for the children and they can get firsthand experience. Such trips include visit to red cross hospitals. Clinics, fairs exhibitions, yogic center public health center and water supply centers etc. however each visits needs proper planning and advance class room discussion to motivate young children. At the end of visit if the teacher clarifies the doubts of the students it will be more beneficial for the children.

9. Health Weeks

It is a good method of imparting health instruction to the young pupils. Health week may be celebrated in the school every year in which emphasis is laid on personal hygiene and upkeep of the school campus. Special talks by the expert may be arranged on personal hygiene and sanitation.

10. Health Club

Each institution should organize a health club as self-governing unit. Through this club the students can be associated with institution health laws and their administration. They can also be encouraged to practice health rules in their daily lives. These clubs in co-operation with the institutions Red Cross society should arrange debates declamations plays and dreams on makers concerning health.

11. Health Scrap Books

Students should be encouraged to maintain scrap books on health on the top of every page one important health rule should be written or pasted. Pictures illustrating important health rules, causes and prevention of various disease neat and healthy living functions of various organs in human body should be collected this book should contain the records concerned with the students.

HEALTH SERVICE

The health service programme includes different protective measures to maintain and improve health. Ultimate goal of the institutional health services programme is the attainment of physical mental and emotional health of every student to the optimum experience for students leading them to adopt desirable health habits.

The quality and the quantity of mental work depends upon the conditions of human body. It is not in proper order, optimum output cannot be expected.

Aim

Health services aim of the locating ill health and provide medical care after proper medical checkup.

Agencies of school health services

a.   School Medical Department under the charge of a school Doctor

b.   School health Educator

c.   School Dispensary

d.   Red Cross unit of the School

e.   Sports Department under the charge of a qualified physical education instructor

Programme of health Services

In order to ensure normal and sound physical condition of the students, the institutions should establish certain organized services and the programme should constitute.

Medical Inspection and maintaining Records

☐ Proper arrangements in the school to get every student medically examined at the time of his first admission to the institution and in subsequent years

☐ Periodically arrange for health inspection of the pupils with regard to vision hearing dental health and personal hygiene.

☐ Maintain the records of medical inspection and health status of the children

☐ Promote the importance of vaccination and immunization to parents of words.

☐ If any dangerous disease is identified the school authorities should proper steps and suggest the parents of wards to consult the experts in the hospital.

Duties of teachers

Observation by the teacher and experts to locate defects and disease if any especially of skin, eyes, ears, teeth etc in the wards inform in the parents for speed recoveries.

In addition, teachers should look at the child's posture. Cleanliness and hygienic conditions. If they observe any deformity or diseases in the pupils they must inform the school doctor and check that the treatment at the clinic is carried out whole time dispenser should be appointed for the school clinic of dispensary where children may be given proper first aid and medicines for small diseases and for some ailments.

School clinic

A school clinic or dispensary needs proper care and should be equipped with medicines for ordinary aliment dispensary tables, chairs, charts and models concerning health, bed for the sick of patients, scale for measuring height, covered dustbin, heater and first aid boxes etc.

A school clinic helps in looking after the health of the pupils and for the systematic treatment of small diseases. There should be at least two rooms for school clinics or dispensary out of which one should be reserved for the school doctor were the pupils consult the doctor about their personal problems

Follow up work

Head of the institutions may arrange for timely vaccination against small box and typhoid so as to reduce outbreak of this infectious diseases.

If some students have some contagious disease like ring worm eczema or leprosy precautionary measures should be adopted till they cured of such diseases

The health status of the students reading in the school be appraised annually

The physical defects of the children should be corrected All the students of the school should get the benefit school health counseling

The guidance personnel physicians school health educators and the teachers should interpret to student and their parents the nature and significance of health problems and help them in formulating plans of action leading to the solution of the problems of the students.

UNIT-3

III METHODS, ORGANISATION AND ADMINISTRATION

3.1 Methods of Teaching Physical Education.

3.2 Intramural and Extramural Competitions.

3.3 Camping - Definition and Meaning – Scope and significance of Camping.

3.4 Warming up: Types of Warming up - Importance of warming up.

3.1 Methods of Teaching Physical Education

Various methods may be adopted for teaching physical activities.

1. Command Method

Usually formal activities are taught by command method where certain words of command are used to obtain the required position This is of two types (viz) Response Command & Rhythmic Command. To teach an exercise, Response Command is used where each position of the exercise is to be held and the accuracy and the precision of the position are to be emphasized. The Rhythmic Command is used when the exercise already taught is to be repeated rhythmically for physiological results. Here, emphasis is on movements and not on held positions.

2. Oral Method

In this method the teacher merely explains the activity by words without any demonstration and expects the class to perform it. (This method of teaching is not wholly desirable).

3. Demonstration Method

Here the teacher will demonstrate the activity with a brief f explanation. The students have to observe the teacher's demonstration and then perform the activity on the command of the teacher. This is the most high1y recommended method of teaching.

4. Imitation Method

This is adopted when an activity is one that was already taught or an activity which can be easily followed. In this case the teacher says "Follow me" or "Do as I do" When the teacher leads an activity and then changes the movements, the boys perform the same by imitation.

5. Dramatization Method

In this method the pupils are made to perform the movements of animals. birds, motor cars, trains airplanes, soldiers, sailors etc., story plays and action songs in play form. There is a lot of scope for exhibiting the imagination of the pupils. This method is most suitable for the children of the elementary grades.

6. At-Will Method

In this method the students are given an opportunity to perform the activity in their own time and rhythm. In other words, this is a free form of exercising.

7.Set – Drill Method

This method will consist of a series of well-planned exercises of free arm type and exercises with light apparatus (dumb-bells, clubs, wands, poles etc.) There exercises are memorized and done rhythmically. not only for physiological effects but also for demonstrative values.

8. Whole Method

This method is adopted whenever an activity is to be taught as a whole action without breaking it into its component parts. For example, the teaching of an athletic event like High Jump which includes a series of movements (viz. approach, take-off, lay-out and landing) is done by this method. Even though each of these movements may be analyzed and emphasized.

9. Part Method

This is adopted whenever a particular activity is broken into its meaningful parts and taught; for example, the teaching of the individual skills of a major game.

10. Whole-Part- Whole Method.

In this method a full and clear conception of the whole activity is given at the outset. Then the activity is divided into its meaningful parts and taught.; after practicing these parts as separate skills they are put in a practice game situation Thus initial practice is on the individual parts. Then the parts are combined into the whole activity. This method is highly recommended to teach a major game. The following examples will clearly indicate what may be meant as a WHOLE or as a PART.

Whole Activity	*Its Meaningful Parts*
i Game of Football (Soccer)	Kicking, Dribbling etc.
ii Kicking the Football	Approach, planting of the standing leg, the swing of the kicking leg, proper contact with the ball, follow through etc.

11. Progressive Part Method:

This method is to be adopted usually to teach rhythmic activities which require a lot of co-ordination in this method, the activity is taught step. At the outset step I will be taught: then step 2: afterwards steps 1 &2 will be combined. Thereafter step 3 will be taught and steps 1, 2 & 3 will be combined in this manner all the steps of the activity will be taught in a progressive manner Finally the whole activity will be performed with proper co-ordination. This method of teaching is called the progressive part method. This method is also adopted to teach Track & Field athletics.

12. Observation and Visualization Method.

Student, whenever opportunity arises, may be taken to places where Champion Teams and Athletes compete (eg State, National Competition etc.) so that they can observe them in action and learn some of the finer tactics. Observe them in action and learn some of the finer tactics. Strategies and technique of games and the events,

Films, preferably in slow motion, depicting the finer points of the activity may be repeatedly shown with due comments so that effective learning may take place.

3.2 Intramural and Extramural Competitions.

Intramural Competitions

"Intramural" means **"within the walls"**. Hence Intramural competitions are the competitions held within an institution.

Objectives:

- To develop the skills of the students in the concerned activities.
- To provide incentive for participation in the activities.
- To provide opportunities for hundred percent participation among the homogeneous groups, thereby contributing the greatest good for the greatest number.
- To develop leadership and fellowship qualities.
- To give the best knowledge of the rules of the game and to develop desirable social qualities like co-operation team work, respect for official opponents etc.
- To give fun, pleasure and enjoyment. In training institutions, the following objectives have also to be borne in mind.
- To give experience to the trainees in organizing and conducting the intramural competitions as a part of their training.
- To provide opportunities for the trainees to gain experience in officiating.

Method of Organising and Conducting Intramural Competitions

1. The following factors have to be taken into account in conducting the competitions:
2. Type of the institution (Residential, non-residential, etc.)
3. Local and climatic conditions.
4. Facilities available (Playgrounds, equipment, leadership etc).
5. Finance
6. Time at disposal
7. Activities in which students take major interest.
8. Co-operation and help that can be expected from the colleagues.

Units for Competition:

The students have to be divided into several units for the purpose of competition. The units must be of equal ability and strength. It is better to have 2 or 3 divisions is each unit so that competitions among the highly skilled boys can be separately conducted. The formation of the units depends upon the type of the institution.

1. Purely Residential Institutions:

In this type of institution, competitions can be conducted on Inter-Hostel basis or house basis. It can also be conducted on Wing or Dormitory basis.

2. Partially Residential Institutions:

In this type of institution, the students residing in the hostels will be divided into several teams and the day scholars will be divided into a few teams. The division of the day scholars into teams may be done on Area basis.

3. Non-residential Institutions:

In this type of institution, the units may be formed in any one of the following ways:

- On class basis, among the particular grades; (i.e.) among the classes in the Middle school stage, the High school stage etc.

- On index basis, students are divided into Seniors Intermediates. Juniors and Sub-Juniors according to their indices. Competitions are conducted among each particular division separately. This is one of the best methods of forming the units because this will be useful for the selection of students, for inter-school competitions.

- In colleges, the units may be either on class basis or on departmental basis.

Intramural Committee:

The conduct of the intramurals is to be given to an intramural committee. This committee will usually consist of the following.

1) The Intramural Director:

He will always be the senior physical education teacher; he will be assisted by the other physical education teachers of whom one may be appointed as an Assistant Director of Intramurals. Further they will be assisted by class-room teachers when competitions are held.

2) The Unit Contains and Vice-Captains:

They will be members of the intramural committee. A Secretary and a Joint-Secretary are to be selected or elected from among these Unit Leaders.

It is the responsibility of this committee to frame rules and regulations for the competitions. It is the duty of the Secretary to keep a record of the meetings held, the results of the competitions and the score sheets, Protests, if any, are the be decided by this committee.

Activities Suitable for Competitions:

All major games, swimming, Track & field, tumbling and pyramids, demonstrations by each unit, defensive arts, rhythmic activities etc., are suitable for competitions. Although most of the above activities can be included in the program, it is better to decide the items in which competitions could be completed within the time at the disposal of the committees.

Time:

Intramural competitions shall be conducted all-round the year. There shall be a heavy program of intramural during the first and the second terms. During the third term these shall be a light program of intramural because of the coming examinations.

The time best suited for competitions is after school hours and on holidays. The competitions may be conducted either on league basis or knock-out basis.

Scoring:

Points shall be awarded for each team of each unit for each activity according to the places they gain. The points gained by a team shall be credited to the unit. There shall be two score sheets, one to enter the points scored by each team in day to day competitions and the other a permanent or consolidated score sheet showing the points gained by each unit. The total points scored by each unit at the end of the competition will decide the intramural champions.

Award:

Some kind of recognition must be given to the winners in each activity and to the intramural champions. Separate shield for each activity and certificates to the winners of each activity may be awarded. The intramural Honour Board and Certificates may be given to the Intramural Champions. A photograph of the Champion Unit may be taken and fixed to the Honor Board.

Points to be borne in mind for encouraging larger participation in intramural Competitions:

1) Fix the units for competition on the basis of the classification obtaining in schools (e.g.) Seniors, Juniors etc., and arrange for competitions separately under each classification.

2) Make the competition fair by arranging for balanced teams in each classified unit. Teams may be classified as A, B and C in each unit for each activity.

3) Eliminate the members of the school's teams from intramural Competitions or distribute them equally to the different intramural competitions or distribute them equally to the different intramural teams.

4) Limit the number of activities in which a student can participate.

5) Arrange for competition in a variety of activities making use of all the facilities of the institution.

6) Award extra points for activities in which the students have less interest.

7) Give extra point for 100% participation.

8) Frame the rules in such a manner that substitutes shall be put into the game for a specified period of time (for example: In the game or Football or Hockey, substitutes shall play, at least, for 10 minutes; in the game of volleyball, substitutes shall play, at least, for 4 points or 4 side outs in a game).

9) Give some award or recognition to the individuals and to the teams winning each activity and also to intramural champion Team.

EXTRAMURAL COMPETITIONS

Extramural competitions are Inter-Institutional competitions. They give an opportunity for the representative members of the teams of the various institutions to exhibit their talents and bring honor to their institutions.

There are a few benefits as well drawbacks in the inter-institutional competitions.

Benefits:

1) The standard of performance of the participants will be improved.

2) Loyalty to the institution is developed.

3)There is ample scope for the development of leadership, followership and sportsmanship qualities.

4) New acquaintances and friendships become possible.

5) The participants acquire a good knowledge of the places they visit.

6) The participants derive pleasure, fun and enjoyment through healthy competitions.

Drawbacks:

1) Sometimes questionable methods are adopted for the sake of victory. Teams try to win by fair or foul means.

2) Unhealthy rivalry and jealousy are created.

3) Too much of time, money and energy are wasted.

4) There is too much of strain on the part of the students.
5) Some of the participants get swollen-headed and exhibit a false pride.

The above drawbacks may be easily rectified through proper leadership discipline among the players must be enforced. However good player may be, if he does not turn up (without valid reasons) for regular training and practice, he shall be excluded from the team. This will have a salutary effect on the players and discipline can be easily maintained. A good leader should teach the participants respect for rules and regulations, officials, opponents etc.

3.3 Camping - Definition and Meaning – Scope and significance of Camping

The history of recreational camping is often traced back to a British travelling tailor, Thomas Hiram Holding, but it was actually first popularized in the UK on the river Thames. By the 1880's large numbers of visitors took part in the leisure time activity, which was also considered as the late Victorian craze for pleasure boating. Thomas Hiram Holding was considered as the father of modern camping in the UK. The form of camping promoted by Thomas was something that he has experienced in the wild from his youth, when he had spent much time with his parents travelling across the American prairies. He later embarked on a cycling as camping tour with some his friends across Ireland, he wrote a book on his Ireland experience Cycle and Camp in Connemara which led to the formation of the first camping group in 1901, the Association of Cycle Campers, later known as the Camping and Caravanning Club. The Association later merged into the National Camping Club. The International Federation of camping Clubs was founded in 1932 with national clubs from all over the world affiliating to it.

Camping is an outdoor recreational activity, which involves an individual to stay outdoors and away from the comforts of his home in a shelter such as a tent, a caravan or a motorhome. The general idea is to take a leave from the developed areas to spend time outdoors in more natural ones in pursuit of activities providing the thrill and enjoyment. For an activity to be considered to be camping it is an essential characteristic that a minimum of one night is spent outdoors, and this feature distinguishes it from activities such as day-tripping, picnics and all other similarly short-term recreational activities.

Leadership is both a research area and a practical skill encompassing the ability of an individual or organization to 'lead' or guide other individuals, teams, organization or an entire country. It is the ability to build up confidence and zeal among people and to create an urge in them to be led. Leadership is an important element in directing the functions of a group, an organization or management. Wherever there is an organized group of people working towards a common goal, some form of leadership becomes essential. "The power of leadership is the power of integrating". A good leader stimulates the best qualities in a group, unites and concentrates scattering. A leader provides a direction or channel for the unused potential to be utilized, thereby increasing the creativity and productivity of the group.

Camping and leadership go hand in hand, while camping provides individuals with the skill sets required to survive in tough situations, leadership is essential that the campers don't lose hope and are directed to work in one direction so as to increase the probability of survival in the wilderness.

Further in the following topics we will be discussing how camps are organized, what are the aims and objectives they sought to fulfill, the importance of camping and the various types of camps that one may participate in depending in the needs of the camper.

Camp can be educational as well as recreational. Further, the modern age has made recreational skills almost as important as educational skills. Down through the centuries, history shows that the greatest care has been given or focused on camping and living in out of doors. The role of camping in one's life is not new in our country. Historically, camping goes back to the dawn of civilization. Camping was at its peak during the Epic Age. In those days' people learnt from one another as they struggled to survive in the outdoor environment.

Modern camps are becoming more democratic, permitting for free participation in activities and in planning of the programme. The interests of campers are ascertained by means of various methods and used as the basis of programme working. The term organization is given to the process of bringing individual elements in a situation into such relationships with each other that they will function as a whole in achieving the central purpose of the institution. Since there are many parts in every camp. The necessity of organisation is immediately to function effectively for the achievement of its purposes.

Meaning of A Camp

The dictionary meaning of a camp is "a place where people, students, troops etc. live for a specific time in tents or huts". Further it may be implied that camp means living together in a group away from the homes, institutions, hostels etc. for outdoor education.

Outdoor education was a primary educational technique of the Greek Era. Before the Roman Empire entered its period of decline, it had the most extensive and highly organized system of education that the world had ever known. The term outdoor education and camping are used synonymously.

Aim and Objectives of the Camps

Aim of the Camper

The camper's aim in attending camps is "Fun'. A Camper judges every activity on the basis of pleasure and interest. To fail to satisfy the camper's aim will disastrously defeat the central aim of a camp.

The camp must be recreational to the extent that it must be satisfying to camper's aim but it does not prevent from doing a very high level of educational work. Every sown definite objectives and goals, towards which every phase of camp life will camp has its be directed.

Objectives of a Camp

The following are the most common and important objectives of a camp:

1. To further the welfare of campers and its leaders, through camping /outdoor education.
2. To extend the recreational and educational benefits of outdoor living.
3. To give stress in camping on leadership and citizenship training in keeping with the principles and traditions of democracy.

4. To give more opportunities for spiritual development through camping.
5. To provide opportunities for developing fellowship among the campers.
6. To stimulate high professional/educational standards of camp leadership.
7. To provide for exchange of experiences and successful practices, and for development of materials, standards and other aids for the progress of camping.
8. To interpret camping to related groups and to the public.
9. To develop the skill of improvisation in the absence of real things/material.
10. To provide opportunities to develop better understanding among themselves which enhances socialization.

Organization of Camping

A camping trip may be the highlight of the year for lots of groups. These are the few days or 2-3 weeks of rich experiences and things to be done together with peers or people of the same interests away from the protective atmosphere of our home and also away from the watchful eyes of parents for some. Planning such an event and seeing it through is a challenge for each group leader. The growth of the group and form bonds with other members works best in camps. They are together as a group for several days; no one has the option to run away in between camps. Doing things together pushes people together and forms bonds. Since camps are away from home and so an individual gets used to new situations, do without their daily shower and sleep in a place which is not as comfortable as the soft bed back at home. Independence, social behavior, helping out and dealing with disagreements might be totally new experiences for some kids.

In order to make it an experience of a lifetime and that they keep coming back for more there are certain aspects that need to be considered. Before organizing a camp, the following general things needs consideration:

- o An adequate and competent camp personnel

- Budgeting
- Target group
- Camp site
- Food and refreshments
- Equipment supply
- Program/activities/contents
- Daily program/activity schedule
- Duration of the camp
- Transportation of the campers
- Plan of the camp site
- Pitching and allotment of tents
- Grouping of students
- Health
- Sanitation and safety
- Records
- Fees
- Rules of the camp
- Problems of the camp

Scope and Significance of Camping

We all are aware that camping is a fantastic recreational activity, providing hours of enjoyment and a welcome opportunity to connect with loved ones, other campers, as well as nature. But that's just the start. Camping also has a whole range of wonderful health benefits, from physical and mental aids to those that are tailor made for children, these benefits ensure there's even more reason to involve in camping activities. Following are the importance of camping:

1. Camping helps with problem solving:

Camping and the activities associated with it present the camper with challenges which he needs to solve at that very instant. The challenges are not something that one comes across in daily life like where and how to set up your tent; or how to deal with scenarios where one cannot use the modern gadgets or items of familiarity. In addition to all of the above, camping introduces the camper to new experiences – perhaps an activity he always wanted to try but never found time for. Whatever the case, new challenges and experiences keep your brain healthy, as they force you to think for yourself. Outdoor education awakens the people to a whole new world of new ideas, which tends to give them a deep and affectionate respect of life.

2. Camping is great for children's education:

Camping introduces children and individuals to a whole new world and asks them an ability to overcome new problems and challenges, having exposure to a different set of challenges not only keeps the brain healthy but leads to increased learning opportunities. Outdoor education is a method of education through direct experience with nature, people, objects, places and actually 'Learning by Doing'. Learning is faster when it is done practically and has a prolonged effect, there is also a greater appreciation and understanding for those things that are learned first-hand.

3. Camping helps you sleep better:

Another important benefit of camping is that it is good for health, especially for people suffering from sleep disorder or lack of sleep. Research in 2013 from the University of Colorado Boulder found that camping can re-set our biological clock and help those of us who find it tough to sleep and/or wake up in the morning. It is particularly due to the increased use of artificial light in our daily lives and the fact that camping can help us to adjust to the natural light-dark cycle if we're given that chance. Receiving adequate sleep has long been touted as critical to our overall health and wellbeing.

4. Camping increases your vitamin D intake

As camping is an outdoor activity hence that chances to spend more time under the open sky, but in order to get all the Vitamin D it is essential to be under the sun at the right time.

5. Camping leads to increased exercise:

It generally happens that our daily routine entails long sitting hours in the office or at home with kids; the chances for exercises are very limited. Going for camping is a great opportunity to explore new surroundings; wandering through a nearby national park or even mountain climbing. This increased exercise has myriad physical and mental benefits, which also includes combatting health problems and diseases thereby improving quality of life.

6. Camping makes you happier:

As camping lightens up the mood and improves the quality of life. It's

all to do with serotonin, the chemical that our body produces that helps to make us happy. It has be studied that some factors that help the body create serotonin comprises of: more sunlight, more oxygen and increased physical activity and camping ticks all the boxes.

Types of Camp

There are various types of camping some of them are:

- ➢ Adventure Camping
- ➢ Dry Camping
- ➢ Backpacking
- ➢ Canoe Camping
- ➢ Bicycle Camping
- ➢ Car, Off-Road and RV
- ➢ Glamorous Camping or Glamping
- ➢ Reenactment Camping
- ➢ Social Camping
- ➢ Urban Camping
- ➢ Winter Camping
- ➢ Work Camping

All camps are different from each other, some are far superior to others because of the type of personnel they employ, the facilities they possess and the services they render. There are boys' camps, girls' camp as well as co-ed camps. Co-ed camp is often selected when there are boys and girls of a specific age for a specific camp and where there is a need from the professional institutions to train both the genders for the professional career.

There are various types of camps and sometimes with specific themes such as music, drama, horse riding, training camps for games and sports, work camps (N.S.S. camps), religious camps, institutional camps (school, college or university etc.), camps for the specially abled, youth camps etc.

Sometimes they may be simply categorized into the following three as well:

1. Co-ed Camps: As mentioned above as well these camps are common for both genders.

2. Non-Private Camps: These are also called organizational or institutional camps. They may vary in their operations. Some of these camps operate for a full summer season with fees as high as private camps.

3. Boys Scout Camps and Girls Guide Camps.

Camping is one of the most entertaining outdoor recreation program attracting huge groups of people of different age groups, there are various types of camps being organized for different groups with a wide range of themes. However, it is the camp organizers who have to take care of a lot of aspects so as to make this a life time experience and also that the participants are satisfied when they go back to their daily lives. Their productivity should improve and they would not only come back for another camping experience but also bring more of their friends or family with them.

3.4 Warming up: Types of Warming up - Importance of warming up.

Suppose you are told that you have to add an extra five to 10 minutes to warm-up can have a many beneficial effects on your workout and thus, your overall health. So any exercise sessions must start with warm up and end with a cool down.

It is a primarily preparatory activity in which through physiological and psychological preparation, a player/athlete adjusts himself for the fulfilment of the main activity.

Types of Warming Up

1. General Warming up – In general warming up, athlete/player goes through a series of physical movements of general nature for the whole body such as jogging, striding, stretching, calisthenics.

2. Specific Warming up – In specific warming up, athletes go through such movements which are to be performed later on the main activity are competition such as sprinter may go through short distance run; Volleyball player may prepare his joints for main activity; Hockey player with stick and ball may goes through the skill which he has to perform later on in the main activity

What Happens in Our Body?

When we start to exercise, our cardio respiratory and neuromuscular systems and metabolic energy pathways are stimulated. Muscles contract, and to meet their increasing demands of oxygen, our heart rate, blood flow, cardiac output and breathing rate increase. Blood moves faster through our arteries and veins and is slowly routed to working muscles. Our body temperature rises and oxygen is released more quickly raising the temperature of the muscles. This allows the muscles to use glucose and fatty acids to burn calories and create energy for the exercises. All of these processes prepare the body for higher intensity action.

Significance of Warming Up

1. It raises the core body temperature, which improve physical work efficiency.
2. It increases the stroke volume as per demand of muscles to be used in the activity.
3. It also increases the lung ventilation, which supplies more oxygen.
4. It results in the removal of lactic acid, which helps in improving the endurance.
5. It enables to reduce the chances of feelings of stretch in the side.
6. It helps the athlete to enjoy the second wind at the earliest possible.
7. It improves agility.
8. It improves reaction time.
9. It improves co-ordination.
10. It improves the range of motion (ROM) in the joints.
11. Players /athletes get used to the ground/surface condition more especially through specific warming up.
12. Players/athletes get used to the environments mainly the crowed consciousness or light condition if there are artificial.
13. It reduces tension and nervousness.
14. It improves the concentration requires for the main task.
15. General and specific warming up results in better skill performance.

General Guidelines That Govern the Warming Up Programme

1. Duration of main activity.
2. Age of the athletes/players.
3. Condition of the players-body or general condition mainly physical fitness.
4. Weather condition and the time of the competition, e.g. early morning, cold, hot, high altitude etc.

Methods of Warming Up

1. Active - Through physical participation procedures, which involve either utilizing the skill or activity that will be used during competition (specific warm-up) or stretching and calisthenics (General warm-up).

2. Passive – passive warming up does not involve physical exercises. Instead, it involves external stimulus such as massage, steam bath, diathermy, whirlpool baths and other such means through which physiological changes take place.

Duration of Warming Up

Duration of warming up depends upon level of training state and level of competition experience. Generally warming up of 15 to 30 minutes is suitable for an activity of 60 to 80 minutes. Warming up of 5 to 10 minutes is enough for untrained players or beginners.

Components of Warming Up

Warming up can be done through three main components

(1) stretching (2) Calisthenics/ flexibility and (3) formal activity.

1. Stretching – After having progressive aerobic activity like slow jogging which uses the muscles one will be during exercise sessions, stretching should follows. While performing stretching major muscle and joints should be used but without any jerking. Stretching prepares the muscular skeletal tissues for vigorous movements. Warmed up muscles need to elongated to make them supple and elastic.

2. Calisthenics/ flexibility exercises- After stretching one should go for calisthenics or flexibility exercises. All such exercises should be performed in a sequence, gradual manner and whole-body parts be involved.

3. Formal activity – Final phase of warming up should be related to the main activity. You must perform some activities relating to main workout in a slow manner. For example, if you will be running, warm up with a slow jog, or if you will be cycling then begin in lower gears. Formal activity relating to main task may be performed with or without equipment like bowling action without ball or with ball. Knocking racquet sports.

Physiological Basis of Warming Up

Warming up enhances the body core temperature. If the core temperature of the body is increased by 1 c then basal metabolic rate (bmr) is increased by 14% thus enhance the physical work capacity. Consequently, Haemoglobin(RBC) carries more oxygen, which resulted; more oxygen exchange between blood/tissue and myoglobin tissues.

During warming up propagation of nerve impulses became faster which improves and sharpens the reaction time Rate of contraction of muscle becomes faster as the viscosity is lowered. Thus the chances of injuries or wear and tear are minimized Because of these physiological adaptation physical work capacity is increased through warm up.

COOLING DOWN

Lowering down the intensity of the work out/training session/competition by performing limbering and stretching exercises followed by deep breathing relaxation exercises is called cooling down or limbering down.

Significance of cooling down

When we exercise there is a lot of blood flow in our muscles if we stop suddenly there may be pooling of blood in the extremities and cause giddiness and sometime collapse. Cooling down exercises release the extremity blood into circulation and make the exchange easier. Cooling down exercises prevent the post exercise soreness a stiffness.

Cooling down is essential for recovering to pre-exercise/workout state and for readjusting various functions i.e. physical physiological, bio chemical and Psychological. Cooling down is also essential to avoid pooling down of blood in veins, which causes fatigue.

Free Hand Stretching Exercise for Warming Up and Cooling Down

The following are examples of general stretching and flexibility exercises. Each exercise comprises of a photograph and details of how to perform the exercise. The exercises could for part of the warming up and cooling down elements of a training session.

1. Shoulder Circles

- Stand tall with good posture
- Raise you right shoulder towards your right ear, take it backwards, down and then again with a smooth rhythm
- Perform this shoulder circling; movement eight times, then repeat with the other shoulder
- Breathe easily throughout

2. Arm Circles:

- Stand tall with good posture.
- Lift one arm forward then take it backwards in a continuous circling motion, keeping your spine long throughout.
- Avoid the tendency to arch your spin whilst carrying out the circling movement.
- Perform this arm circling movement eight times, before repeating with the other arm.
- Breathe easily throughout.

3. Side Bends:

- Stand tall with good posture, feet slightly wider than shoulder width apart, knees slightly bend, hands resting on hips.
- Lift your trunk up and away from your hips and bend smoothly first to one side, then the other, avoiding the

tendency to lean either forwards or backwards.

➢ Repeat the whole sequence sixteen times with a slow rhythm, breathing out as you bend to the side, and in as you return to the center.

4. Trunk Twists:

➢ Stand tall with good posture.

➢ Have your feet slightly wider than hip-width apart, knees slightly bend, hands resting on hips.

➢ Keeping your spine long and your hips facing forward, turn smoothly and slowly round to one side, then the other.

➢ Repeat the sequence sixteen time, breathing easily throughout the movement.

5.   Upper Back Stretch:

➢ Stand or sit tall with posture.

➢ If standing bend your knees slightly and tilt your pelvis under.

➢ Interlock your and fingers and push your hand as far away from your chest as possible allowing your upper back to relax whilst at the same time looking down.

➢ You will feel the stretch between your shoulder blades

➢ Hold the stretch for 20 seconds breathing easily throughout.

6. Chest Stretch:

➢ Standing bend your knees and tilt your pelvis under.

➢ Pace your hands loosely clasped on the small of your back and keep your spine long and shoulder back and away from your ears.

➢ Without arching your spine, ease your elbows towards each other as far as possible, feeling the stretch in the front of the chest.

➢ Hold the stretch for 20 seconds, breathing easily throughout.

7.Standing Side Bend:

> Make sure that you have a good stable base by placing your feet approximately a meter apart, toes facing forward.
> Bend your knees slightly and keep your hips facing forward, too.
> Hold the stretch for 20 seconds, breathing easily throughout.
> Repeat on the other side.

8. Sideways Neck Stretch:

> Stand or sit tall with good posture, keeping your spine and neck long and your shoulder down away from your ears.
> Keeping your neck long, tilt your head to the side.
> Hold the stretch for 20 seconds, breathing easily throughout.
> Repeat on the other side.

9. Front of shoulder stretch

> Sit on a stool tall with good posture, bend your knees slightly and tilt your pelvis under.
> Place your hands behind you, interlock your fingers and then straighten your arms and try and lift them upwards and backwards as far as possible.
> Keep your spine long throughout and make sure that your shoulders are back and down away from your ears.
> You will feel the stretch in the front of the chest.
> Hold the stretch for 20 seconds, breathing easily throughout.

10. Front of shoulder stretch

> Sit on stool or stand tall with good posture, bend your knees slightly and tilt your pelvis under.
> Place both hands above your head and then place your right hand behind your head, easing the left arm closer towards your head taking the elbow behind the head if possible.
> Keep your spine long and your shoulders down away from your ears throughout the exercise.
> You will feel the stretch along the side of the trunk and

shoulder.

- ➢ Hold the stretch for 20 seconds, breathing easily throughout.
- ➢ Repeat on the opposite side.

11. Half Squat

- ➢ Stand tall with good posture holding your hands out in front of you for balance.
- ➢ Now bend at the knees until your thighs are parallel with the floor.
- ➢ Keep your back long throughout the movement, and look straight ahead.
- ➢ Make sure that your knees always point in the same direction as your toes.
- ➢ Once at your lowest point, fully straighten your legs to return to your starting position.
- ➢ Repeat the exercise sixteen times with a smooth, controlled rhythm.
- ➢ Breath in as you descend, and out as you rise.

12. Standing

- ➢ Stand tall with one leg in front of the other, hands flat and at shoulder height against a all or suitable immovable object.
- ➢ Ease your back leg further away from the wall, keeping it straight and press the heel firmly into the floor.
- ➢ Keep your hips facing the wall.
- ➢ You will feel the stretch in the calf of the rear leg.
- ➢ Hold the stretch for 20 seconds, breathing easily throughout.
- ➢ Repeat on the other side.

13. calf Stretch

- ➢ Position yourself as for the standing calf stretch exercise.
- ➢ This time, however, flex the knee of the rear leg, whilst still keeping the heel pressed firmly on to the floor.
- ➢ The sensation of stretch for 20 seconds, breathing easily throughout.

> Hold the stretch for 20 seconds, breathing easily throughout.
> Repeat on the other side.

14. Standing Hip and Thigh Stretch

> Stand tall with good posture in front of a firm chair or stool.
> Raise one foot up on to the chair back easing your body towards this foot so that chest and thigh come closer together.
> Rest your hands loosely on the raised knee and keep your spine and back leg straight and your shoulders down away from your ears.
> Ease as far forward as possible and hold your position.
> You will feel the stretch along the front of the thigh of the extended leg, and along the back of the thigh of the raised leg.
> Hold the stretch for 20 seconds, breathing easily throughout.
> Repeat on the other side.

15. Seated Groin Stretch

> Sit tall with good posture.
> Ease your legs up towards your body and place the sole of your feet together, allowing your knees to ease out down towards the floor.
> Make sure that your back stays long and that your shoulders are down away from your ears.
> Rest your hands on your lowers leg or ankles, or keep them away by your sides for support
> Your will feel that stretch along the inside of your things and groin If you wish to stretch the hamstrings and hip extensors at the same time, from the position above ease forward by hinging at the hip, still keeping the spine long
> Hold the stretch for 20 seconds, breathing easily throughout

16. Kneeling Hip Flexor Stretch:

> Kneel on a mat or towel with one leg flexed in front of your

as illustrated-your weight should be evenly distributed so that you position is stable, although you can use your hands at either side of your body for extra support

> ➤ Note that the knee at the front leg is positioned directly over the front foot
> ➤ From this position and keeping your spine long and shoulders down, push your hips forward
> ➤ You may; find that you have to take our rare knee further back before you can feel the stretch along the front of this thigh
> ➤ Hold the stretch for 20 seconds, breathing easily throughout
> ➤ Repeat on the other leg

17. Lying Hip Abductor Stretch:

> ➤ Lie flat on the floor with both legs flexed at the knee
> ➤ Now cross your legs and use the weight of the top leg to bring the lower leg down towards the floor
> ➤ Keep your back, shoulders and the foot of the lower leg in contact with the floor throughout the movement
> ➤ You will feel the stretch along the outside of the hip and thigh
> ➤ Hold the stretch for 20 seconds, breathing easily throughout
> ➤ Repeat with other leg

18. Front of Trunk Stretch:

> ➤ Lie down on the floor, fully outstretched.
> ➤ Slide your arms to the sides of your body for support, and ease your chest off the floor, keeping your spine long and your hips firmly pressed into the ground.
> ➤ You will feel the stretch in the front of the trunk.
> ➤ Hold the stretch for 20 seconds, breathing easily throughout.

19. Seated Trunk Twist:

> ➤ Sit all with good posture, legs stretched out in front of you, spine long, shoulders down away from your ears.
> ➤ Place your right leg over your left leg as illustrated and rotate

your trunk, using your left arm against you right knee to help ease you further round.

> Use your right arm on the floor for support.
> You will feel the stretch along the length of the spine as well as in the muscles around the right hip.
> Hold the stretch for 20 seconds, breathing easily throughout.

20. Seated Groin and Hamstring Stretch:

> Sit tall with both legs fully outstretched.
> Flex your right knee so that the right foot rests comfortably along your left inner thigh, with the right knee as close as possible to the floor.
> Keeping your spine long and your shoulders down away from your ears, hinge forward from the hips to reach towards your flexed left foot.
> Go as far forward as possible, and then relax your spine to reach even further forward, holding this stretch position.
> You will feel the stretch along the back of the outstretched leg, and along the inside and rear of the flexed leg.
> Hold the stretch for 20 seconds, breathing easily throughout
> Repeat with the other leg.

21. Lying Quadriceps Stretch:

> Lie face down on the floor, resting your forehead on your right hand.
> Press your hips firmly into the floor and bring your left foot up towards your buttocks, easing it closer to them with your right hand.
> You will feel the stretch along the front of the thigh.
> Hold the stretch for 20 seconds, breathing easily throughout.
> Repeat on the other side.

22. Lying Hamstring Stretch:

> Lie flat on the floor with your knees flexed to approximately

ninety degrees.

➢ Raise your left leg, grasping it loosely behind the thigh with both hands.

➢ Now ease this leg as close to your chest as possible.

➢ You will feel the stretch along the back of the flexed thigh.

➢ Hold the stretch for 20 seconds, breathing easily throughout.

➢ Repeat with the other leg.

References

1. Bucher, C.A., (1964). Foundations of Physical Education, New York: Mosby and Company

2. Atwal & Kansal, (2003) A Textbook of Health, Physical Education and Sports, Jalandhar, A.P. Publisher.

3. Kamlesh. M.L. & Sangral, M.S (1986) Methods in physical Education, Ludhiana : Prakash Brothers

4. Kaur, Manjeet,(2003) Health and Physical Education Ludhiana: Tendon Publications.

5. Singh, Ajmer & Gill, Jagtar Singh and Brar, Racchpal Singh and Bains, Jagdish and Rathee, NirmaljitKaur,(2003) Essentials of Physical Education, Ludhiana : Kalyani Publishers.

6. Kamlesh Sangari : History and Principles of Physical Education.

7. Reema, K. (1996). Physical fitness. New Delhi: Khel Sahitya Sports Publication.

8. Ramachandran, L.T., & Dharmalingam. (1993). Health education. A new approach. NewDelhi: Vikas Publishers Ltd.

9. Charles, B. A. (1992). Foundation of physical education and sport. New Delhi: B1 Publication.